Wallpapering

in a weekend

Wallpapering

in a weekend

Anthony Evans

MEREHURST

This book is dedicated to Valerie, not only for her input into its creation, but also for her general encouragement and support throughout.

Acknowledgements

My thanks must first go to Jane Gordon-Clark of Ornamenta, who so kindly put my name forward to Merehurst.

Thank you to Tim Imrie for the fantastic photographs he took for the projects, as well as for all the lunches in his studio. Thank you also to the staff at Merehurst for their professional advice as well as their considerable patience.

For his technical expertise, thanks to Tony Jenkins, who helped with all aspects of pasting and hanging the wallpapers used in the projects.

Thanks to Jenny Robertson, for allowing her house to be filled with photographic paraphernalia when we wallpapered her staircase.

A big thank you to the wallpaper manufacturers, who so generously supplied the wallpapers, borders, adhesive and paint used in the projects, as well as the photographs of their products for the 'Inspirations' pages. Finally, thank you to The Wallfashion Bureau for allowing us to reproduce their chart 'How many rolls of wallpaper do I need?' on page 14.

First published in 2000 by Merehurst Limited,
Ferry House, 51–57 Lacy Road, London SW15 1PR

Copyright © 2000 Merehurst Limited
Photographs © Merehurst Limited, except those listed below:
Crowson Fabrics: p8 (below left), p10 (above); Lucinda Symons/Robert Harding Picture Library: p8 (below right); Nouveau Fabrics Ltd: p11 (below); Osborne & Little: p9 (above and below), p11 (above)

ISBN 1 85391 867 9

A catalogue record for this book is available from the British Library.

Commissioning Editors: Natasha Martyn-Johns, Anna Sanderson
Design & Art Direction: Fay Singer
Project Editor: Rowena Curtis
Photographer: Tim Imrie
Stylist: Valerie Evans
Illustrations: Michael A. Hill
Production Manager: Lucy Byrne
Publishing Manager: Fia Fornari
CEO & Publisher: Anne Wilson
Marketing & Sales Director: Kathryn Harvey
International Sales Director: Kevin Lagden

Colour separation by Colourscan, Singapore
Printed in Singapore by Tien Wah Press

Contents

Introduction

Home decoration has been a spectacular growth area for a decade, but it is only in the last two or three years that wallpaper has come firmly back into fashion. This is an exciting development, as there are few, if any, forms of decoration that offer so much satisfaction and lasting value for money.

One reason for this resurgence of interest in wallpaper is that the manufacturers have done their homework and really taken notice of what people want. After all those dreary browns and greens of the 1970s (although it is still possible to find these colours) there is now a staggering wealth of pattern and colour available from which to choose. At the same time the growing numbers of magazines, books and television programmes about interior decoration and design have encouraged us all to be much more imaginative and adventurous in the way we decorate our homes.

Above all, wallpaper has so much more to offer than paint. Nowadays many people are looking for ways in which to alter the feel or atmosphere of a room, to brighten up a dull area or perhaps even to help create a greater sense of space in a small room or narrow corridor. Or they may just want something a little more 'dressed' and personal than plain paint. Wallpaper, with its myriad patterns, raised designs and combinations of colour, is the ideal solution: it can achieve all these effects, while providing depth and texture, in ways that flat areas of uniform paint cannot.

Some people, however, are still wary of using wallpaper. There is a persistent belief (mainly among those who have not tried) that it is incredibly difficult to put up and that one's first attempts are bound to end in tears. They have visions of ending up covered in paste and tangled up in soggy, crumpled paper or, in cartoon fashion, with pets or children pasted to the walls. It does not have to be like that!

In fact, hanging wallpaper is not only quite straightforward, if approached in a methodical manner, but it is also immensely satisfying and fun to do. This book will take you through the whole process of choosing and applying wallpaper step by step. After the 'Inspirations' section on pages 8–11, explaining how to go about identifying the different effects wallpaper can create and what types of paper would suit your needs, there is a comprehensive guide to all aspects of hanging wallpaper, from the basic equipment needed (remarkably little) and the preparation (very important) to the actual measuring, cutting and hanging. The 'Techniques' section then shows you how to hang wallpaper in every area of the home, including all the tricky bits around doors, fireplaces and ceiling roses.

The central section of the book consists of eight projects, each designed to be completed in a weekend. These range from the use of two wallpapers in a room, to the creation of simple wall panels with a striking three-dimensional effect. Also covered are the techniques of papering a staircase with sloping walls, covering a ceiling and even papering the floor to create the effect of a decorative rug. Another

project shows how to give a number of household items an attractive makeover by covering them with wallpaper. The secret of success with all the projects lies in careful planning and preparation. Not only will this make the completion of each project more satisfying and enjoyable, but it will speed up the process as well.

The projects will introduce you to just some of the many different types of wallpaper that are available and the rich variety of luxurious effects that they can help to create in your home with minimal time and effort.

Enjoy your weekend of wallpapering, which will hopefully be the first of many. If you haven't already discovered how rewarding decorating with wallpaper can be, this could be the weekend in which you begin to transform not only your home but your life! For once you have seen what wallpaper can do, and how easy it is to hang, you may never want to live with plain, painted walls again.

Anthony Evans.

Inspirations

There is no more effective way to transform a home than by the use of wallpaper. Not only can it create any kind of mood, from dramatic to tranquil, but it can be used to make a space feel bigger, warmer, cooler or lighter. It can also hide a multitude of defects. Above all, wallpaper offers an almost infinite number of possibilities of pattern, colour and texture, from the muted to the loud, from a simple striped pattern to a lavish, embossed paper or one that mimics the weave and texture of fabric.

L ong ago, before wallpaper was invented, walls in the grandest homes were covered in woven fabrics, tapestries and leathers, but only a very few could afford this luxury. Even the early wallpapers, which were introduced as a cheaper alternative, were still very expensive compared with those of today. Thanks to the long history of wallpaper, however, there now exists a huge pool of period design for today's manufacturers to dip into.

Indeed the range of designs available is truly mind-boggling – which is what can put some people off! The first way to narrow down the choice is to have a close

Reflect your tastes

No two people have identical taste: some are comfortable with the colours and themes they are used to, while others want to try something new. Wallpaper, with its range of diverse styles and designs, offers something for everyone.

Creating a mood

In the past, wallpapers were designed either for the very young or for the much older, more affluent market. Designers today are finally putting themselves in the shoes of their future customers, and are producing wallpapers and borders for all ages. These wallpapers, like those pictured here, allow customers the opportunity to choose the type of paper they feel will be right for them. Fresh, contemporary patterns such as these are perfect for enlivening a family room or a teenager's bedroom. A folk art-style border adds a charming storyline to the perimeter of a room. If in doubt about a new wallpaper, then pin up a sample to get an idea of what it will be like to live with this design.

A gentler effect for a bedroom has been achieved above by the simple use of a floral border and découpage, where images cut out from the wallpaper have been used to create an attractive, rambling frame on the wall.

A quick makeover

Borders and friezes are the unsung heroes of the wallpaper market, and are able to transform a room, or even an entire home, at minimal cost. Borders can be hung both vertically and horizontally, around windows or doors, as well as applied to household items such as boxes, screens, and lampshades. They can even be placed on walls to make decorative panels. Borders and friezes really do add a touch of drama to any area, and they can be obtained in colours or patterns that will complement exisiting wallpaper or fabric.

Used at a strategic height, borders can also enhance or disguise the size of a room. Confound expectations by replacing the classical lines of picture and dado rails, or cornices, with borders and friezes, for example by hanging a border next to the ceiling in place of a cornice.

look at your home and decide what it is that you want from your wallpaper. Are you after a certain mood, or just a feeling of warmth and comfort? Or do you want to recreate a particular style?

To clarify your thoughts it is well worth spending some time just looking around, to see what excites you. Browse through magazines and books and build up a file of cuttings and photocopies. This will help to identify your preferred styles and to begin your planning.

Much will, of course, depend on the shape, size and function of the room being decorated. If the walls are uneven, you may want to choose a paper with a strong pattern. In rooms with a lot of pictures a quieter design will probably be a better choice. Another deciding factor will be how much a room is used. If you are tempted by a striking, dramatic design, the best place to use it may be in a spare bedroom rather than your living room, for example, where something less busy might be more restful to live with.

The next step is to go to a wallpaper supplier and look through as many books of papers available as possible. Some of the wallpaper sample books have visuals of sets using the various designs, which can be very helpful. Ideally you should have a budget in mind – and sufficient strength of mind to stick to it! However, if you have set your heart on an expensive paper, and cannot find a similar one in a cheaper range, all is not lost. Using a small quantity of one paper in conjunction with another, plainer one, perhaps in the form of stylish panels as in the project shown on pages 56–9, can be just as effective.

Once you have made your choice, just follow the step-by-step instructions in this book and you will be well on your way to producing a wonderful transformation – a beautiful home that has a cohesive look and a professional finish and in which every room feels special.

Contrast and texture

Experiment with different areas of colour and texture, even combining the two in one room. New types of wallcovering are continuously being designed with more luxurious, tactile effects, from fabrics and felts to grasscloth and hessian. It is even possible to get plaster-effect papers, creating a heavily textured look without the mess of applying the plaster.

Create a sense of drama by combining horizontal and vertical stripes, or hang papers strategically to challenge the dimensions of a room. Visually shorten a long room by papering one of the end walls in a vibrant pattern and painting the other walls in a contrasting colour. Remember that strongly patterned papers are harder to hang, and to allow extra paper so that you can match the pattern exactly as you hang.

Fabric and hangings

Fabric, generally a damask made out of silk or linen, has been used as a wallhanging since the seventeenth century. Nothing can beat the rich and luxurious feel of using fabric on a wall.

There are two main methods of applying fabric to a wall; the first is by fixing thin strips of wood, or battens, to the wall, onto which the fabric is attached, the gap between the wall and the fabric having been filled first with a curtain lining. The second, much easier and relatively less expensive way is to send the fabric to a paperbacking company. It can then be hung as a standard wallcovering (see pages 44–5). A paper backing can be applied to almost every available fabric, with the exception of certain silks. Alternatively, there are many, more cost-effective, wallpaper designs with a damask incorporated, as pictured on the right.

However, it is also possible to enjoy the impact of wallpaper without putting it all over a room, either by papering only one wall, or by papering a large panel of plywood and propping it against, or fixing it to, the wall.

Technical information

Do not be alarmed by the process of wallpapering. If everything is done carefully, in a logical order and not hurried, not only will the wallpapering itself be hugely satisfying and fun, but you will end up with a really professional-looking finish.

I t is important to take your time when planning any wallpapering project. It is likely that this part of the process will last weeks or even months, as you explore the various types of wallpaper and wallcoverings available (see the 'Inspirations' section on pages 8–11) and decide how you want to use them.

The basics of successful wallpapering lie in careful preparation. Although this may be time consuming, and it may be tempting to skip this process, it will always pay dividends. The following pages detail every aspect of this all-important preparation process, from choosing the right tools and equipment, how much wallpaper to buy and how to work out the quantities needed, to cutting and pasting the paper. Use this information to suit your room and the type of paper you have choosen to use.

See pages 24–33 for information on all aspects of hanging wallpaper, from hanging a straight drop to papering around doors, windows and other obstacles. Finally, there is advice on using different wallcoverings in the 'Special techniques' section, as well as tips on preventing and solving problems on pages 40–43.

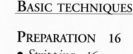

Contents

Selecting wallpaper

Choosing wallpaper means combining personal taste with needs and budget. There are papers which are expensive and not worth the price, and equally there incredibly cheap ones which are best left on the shelf.

Cheap does not always mean good value. It is well worth spending time looking for good quality, value for money wallpapers. There are now a large number of highly professional independent wallpaper shops, as well as department stores and large DIY warehouses that all stock wallpaper. Do not be afraid to ask questions. It is better to be well informed at the beginning of the process rather than to make an expensive mistake at a later stage. Here are a few helpful tips:

COLOUR SAMPLES AND SWATCHES
If you are not sure exactly which colour and pattern of wallpaper you want, take a small piece of existing curtain, upholstery or even carpet from the room, with you to the wallpaper outlet. This will help you and the staff to find the right colour wallpaper.

CREATE A SCRAP BOOK
Similarly, take cuttings or photographs from magazines or colour supplements that have caught your eye with you to help you choose. If the cutting is of a particular wallpaper which has been advertized, it is helpful to have the name and date of the magazine. Try to be as specific as possible.

MEASURE FIRST
Always note the dimensions (height and perimeter) of the room or area which is going to be wallpapered before heading out to the shops. It will then be possible to estimate an approximate number of rolls and a budget can be decided upon.

CHECK DETAILS
Once you have found the right paper, make certain that it is a wallpaper which is not going to be discontinued immediately. This will enable you to order more of the same wallpaper should you need to, or should you decide to use the same paper elsewhere.

A guide to adhesives

Follow the manufacturer's instructions on the wallpaper label when choosing an adhesive. To help avoid any confusion, the following is a guide to the various types of adhesive available:

PREPARED OR TUB PASTE
With prepared paste, no preparation is needed, although it might need some thinning – this depends on the weight of the paper. This paste is very smooth and will hang almost everything.

COLD WATER PASTE
Cold water paste comes in powder form and should be mixed with cold water in a plastic bucket. Follow the directions on the label for quantities. It is easy to mix and is suitable for all kinds of wall and ceiling papers, with the exception of vinyl. Always mix a fresh amount of paste each day.

HOT WATER PASTE
Hot water paste also comes in powder form, and should be mixed with hot water, again following the directions on the label. Allow to cool before using. This paste may be used on all kinds of papers, plus hessians, grasscloths and corks, but not vinyls.

FUNGICIDAL PASTE
Fungicidal paste is especially good for using with vinyl wallpapers (see page 23), because it dries slower than other vinyl adhesives. Do not let children or animals touch or taste this paste and always wash hands after use.

CELLULOSE PASTE
Cellulose paste is a thin, quick setting paste, designed to be used with lighter wallpapers. The advantage of this paste is that it is less likely than others to mark the face of the wallpaper.

OVERLAP ADHESIVE
Stronger than ordinary wallpaper paste, overlap adhesive should only be used for securing wallpaper that is peeling off the wall (see 'Troubleshooting and repairs', pages 40–3).

Hanging vinyl
Vinyl wallpaper should not be hung on new plaster for at least six months, as the vinyl coating stops the plaster from drying out.

Estimating quantities

Start by measuring the room to be decorated. Measure the height and the perimeter, then draw a simple plan of the room showing the doors, windows and the fireplace (see page 15).

Take this plan and the measurements with you when visiting your nearest wallpaper outlet. The staff there should be able to work out the quantity of wallpaper that you will need from these dimensions.

Alternatively, by using the chart here, you should be able work out the number of rolls you will need. To use this chart, follow the numbers down the left hand side, which show the measurement around the room. Then follow the numbers across the top, which show the height. Where the two numbers converge, this will indicate the number of rolls you will require.

However, the chart does not take into consideration doors, windows, recesses and any other features, so cannot be entirely accurate. Always double check your own estimate of how much you need with the wallpaper supplier.

To estimate how much wallpaper you will need to cover the ceiling as well, measure the length and width of the room, then multiply these two figures. If using metric measurements, this will give the total ceiling area in square metres. Divide this figure by five to give the number of rolls needed; one standard roll of wallpaper covers just over 5.4m² (58ft²). A roll of wallpaper (see page 34) is 52cm (21in) wide, and 10m (33ft) long.

HOW MANY ROLLS OF WALLPAPER DO YOU NEED?

DISTANCE AROUND THE ROOM (doors and windows included)	WALLS (height from skirting)						
	2.15-2.30m 7'-7'6"	2.30-2.45m 7'6"-8'	2.45-2.60m 8'-8'6"	2.60-2.75m 8'6"-9'	2.75-2.90m 9'-9'6"	2.90-3.05m 9'6"-10'	3.05-3.20m 10'-10'6"
9m/30'	4	5	5	5	6	6	6
10m/34'	5	5	5	5	6	6	7
12m/38'	5	6	6	6	7	7	8
13m/42'	6	6	7	7	7	8	8
14m/46'	6	7	7	7	8	8	9
15m/50'	7	7	8	8	9	9	10
16m/54'	7	8	9	9	9	10	10
17m/58'	8	8	9	9	10	10	11
18m/62'	8	9	10	10	10	11	12
19m/66'	9	9	10	10	11	12	13
21m/70'	9	10	11	11	12	12	13
22m/74'	10	10	12	12	12	13	14
23m/78'	10	11	12	12	13	14	15
24m/82'	11	11	13	13	14	14	16
26m/86'	12	12	14	14	14	15	16
27m/90'	12	13	14	14	15	16	17
28m/94'	13	13	15	15	15	16	18
30m/88'	13	14	15	15	16	17	19

1

Measuring and planning

Start hanging wallpaper at the focal point of the room. If there is a fireplace, this should generally be your starting point.

1 Find the centre of the fireplace and, using a plumb line, mark a vertical line down the centre of the chimney breast. The first length of paper will then be hung to the right of that line. Hang the remaining wallpaper in a clockwise direction from that point around the room.

2 If there is no fireplace, start papering at a window, working away from the light, in a clockwise direction around the room until reaching the window on the other side. Do not forget to paper above and below the windows.

MEASURING

Using a long steel tape, measure the perimeter of the entire room, including windows, doors and alcoves. Now measure the height of the room from

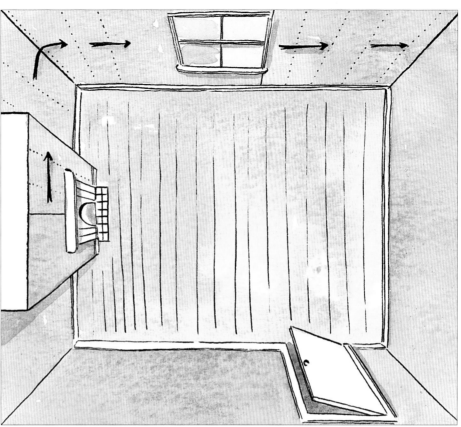

2

the ceiling, or below the cornice if there is one, down to the skirting board. Remember to measure the ceiling if it is going to be papered as well.

USING PATTERNED PAPER

You also need to consider the pattern of the paper when estimating the quantity needed. Wallpaper patterns fall into three basic categories. If there is any doubt about how much to order, always ask the supplier for assistance.

FREE OR RANDOM MATCH
This category includes all plain or striped wallpapers. There is very little wastage with this type of paper as there are no patterns to be matched. Add 10cm (4in) to the top and bottom of each length for trimming.

STRAIGHT MATCH
Papers in this category have a design which lines up horizontally when put

on the wall (see A). These papers result in the most wastage and it is advisable to add one full repeat of the pattern to each length or drop being hung. Add to that 10cm (4in) for trimming.

HALF DROP OR REPEAT
The design on these papers is staggered (see B). To match one drop to the next you will need to drop the design by half a repeat. Add half a repeat to each drop, plus 10cm (4in) for trimming.

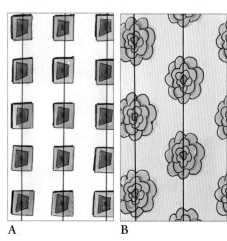

A   B

Basic techniques
Preparation

The most important part of the process of wallpapering, careful preparation is the basis of a well finished result.

STRIPPING

There are two main methods of removing existing wallpaper and the layers of lining paper underneath.

STEAM STRIPPING

Stripping machines are available for sale or for hire from DIY units and tool hire outlets. Make certain that a full set of working instructions are provided. Once it would have been necessary to have strong arms and to wear a mask to use one of these machines but there are now lighter, easy-to-use strippers available.

1 Do not rush when using the stripper and be careful if there is any loose plaster, as even the lightest machine may cause gouges in the wall. Try a small area first to practice on, but once in a rhythm the process will become much easier. Always wear gloves.

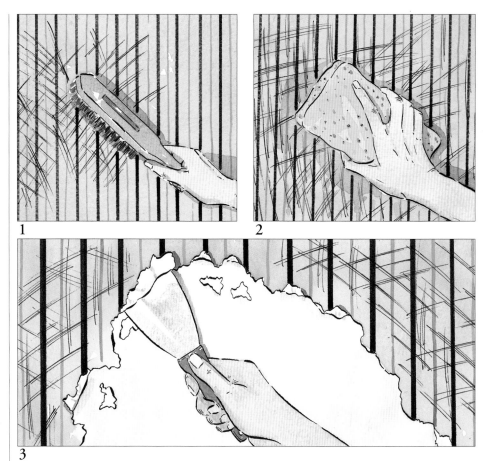

1

Cleaning up

Always make sure your floor is well protected with newspaper or plastic before stripping the walls.

STRIPPING WITH WATER
Although this is possibly a slower and messier way of removing paper than using a machine, it is none the less just as effective. Always try a small area of wall using this method before hiring or buying a stripping machine – more often than not this will be just as effective and will save you money.

1 First, rough up the existing paper on the wall with a wire brush or a proprietary scoring tool.

2 Then apply warm water to the wall, using either a large brush or a sponge. Remember to take up any carpet at the bottom of each wall and cover the floor with plastic sheeting or newspaper, as a mush of wet soggy wallpaper will create a nasty pulpy mess on the floor.

3 Allow the paper to soak for a few minutes, then start removing the paper with a scraping tool, working in small square areas and keeping a strong plastic bag or container close by to put the wet paper into. The longer the wet paper is left on the floor the harder it will be to remove. There are also various proprietary chemical strippers which may be applied direct to the paper or by mixing with water.

STRIPPING VINYLS

Vinyl wallpapers are by far the easiest type of wallpaper to strip.

1 Starting at the bottom, slowly pull the vinyl away from the wall. It is not recommended that the remaining backing paper is left on the wall and it is much better to strip this off too. If it remains, the adhesive used with the new wallpaper may create bubbles and ruin the effect.

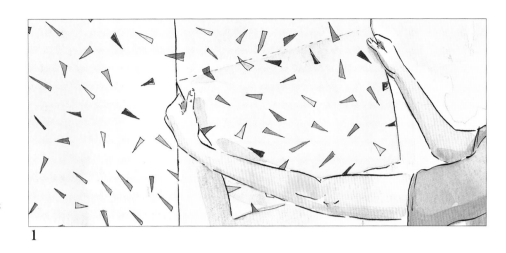

1

Filling, sealing and cleaning

Often stripping off old wallpaper and lining paper will reveal a wall that is less than perfect. Uneven walls need scrupulous filling and cleaning at this stage.

FILLING

Once old wallpaper and any bits of lining paper have been removed it will almost certainly be necessary to do some filling, before any paper, either lining or wallpaper, goes on the wall. In general the places that need attention are internal corners, around doors and windows, above skirting boards and below ceilings.

This can be a tedious job but is well worth the effort if the result is a flawless wall. There are numerous types of proprietary filler available; some ready mixed in a tube, others in powder form which need to be mixed with water.

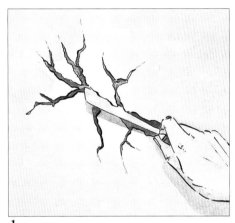

1

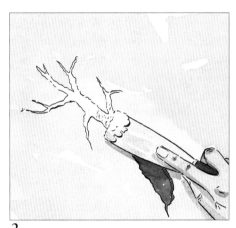

2

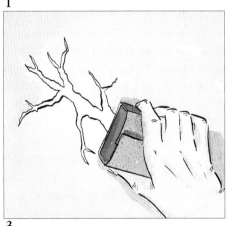

3

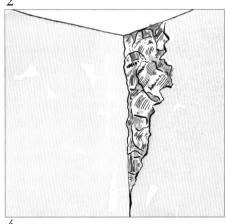

4

1 Before filling, clean out small cracks with a filler knife. Then brush out any loose debris.

2 Smooth filler into the crack with the knife. Flexible fillers are good for cracks around doors, while a fine surface filler should be used on walls.

3 When the filler is completely dry, rub it down to create a smooth surface with a fine-grade sandpaper.

4 Fill the deepest cracks by pushing in some screwed-up newspaper, then fill over the top. Overfill the big cracks – sanding will make the wall even.

Lining paper

There is no doubt that lining the walls prior to hanging wallpaper is essential, even if the walls look smooth and flat without it.

Lining paper is not expensive and it helps create a really good professional finish. The process of putting up the lining paper will also provide some useful practice with hanging paper, and is also a way of finding out if you are likely to encounter any problems when hanging the final wallpaper. Most common complaints and problems with wallpaper are because no lining paper was used.

There are various types and thicknesses of lining paper available. If you have any doubts about which lining paper is right for you, your local wallpaper outlet should be able to help.

There are two ways of hanging lining paper. Horizontally, which is more commonly known as crosslining, or vertically as with standard wallpaper. Crosslining is carried out to ensure that the joins of the lining paper do not line up with the joins of the wallpaper. Although crosslining is a little more difficult than vertical lining, it does become easier with a little practice.

1 To crossline the walls, measure the width of the roll of lining paper (it is slightly wider than standard paper) and measure this distance on the wall using a steel tape measure and mark with a pencil. Start in a corner, working from the ceiling down to the skirting board. Take a spirit level and a straight-edge and make horizontal pencil lines around the room at this distance apart. Cut, paste and fold the paper, following the instructions on pages 21–2.

Applying size

Apply a coat of size or watered-down wallpaper paste all over the walls, and then over the lining paper, using a large brush. This makes a huge difference when the wallpaper is hung, giving 'good slip'; that is, it allows the paper to be moved about as it is being applied to the wall.

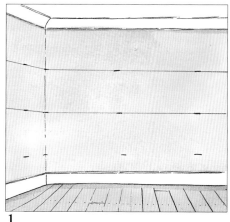

1

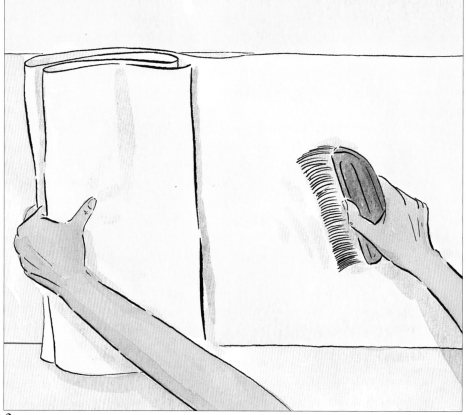
2

3

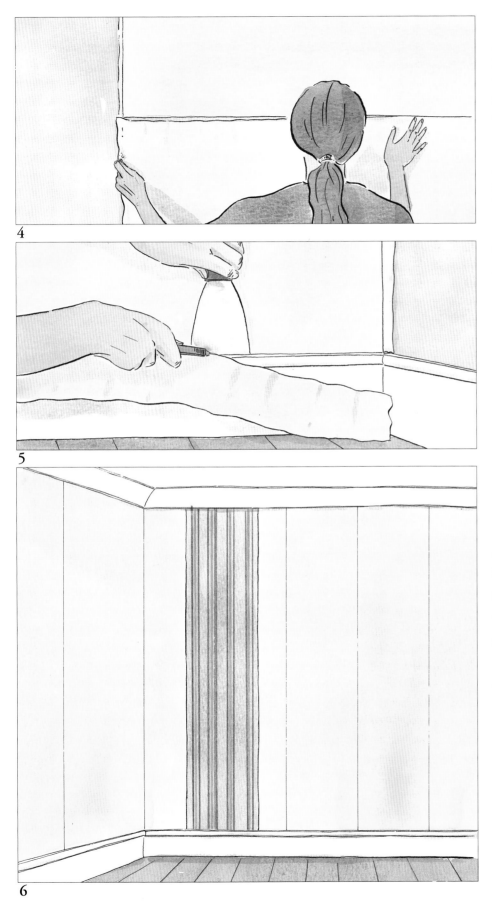

4

5

6

2 Start hanging lining paper from the top of the room. Spread the first length out from one corner, pressing the paper on to the wall with one hand and holding the remaining paper in concertina form with the other.

3 Spread the paper across the wall, continuing around the room. Use a paperhanger's brush to smooth down the paper as you work.

4 Continue hanging the lining paper until you reach the final length, hung near the skirting board.

5 When you reach the skirting board, push the paper down into the angle between the wall and the skirting board. Trim with a craft knife.

6 A professional decorator will nearly always crossline, but it is perfectly adequate to hang the lining paper vertically if doing it yourself. Follow the instructions for hanging wallpaper on pages 24–5. However, you need to ensure that the edges of the lining paper to not correspond with the edges of the wallpaper (see picture).

Damp stains

Damp stains on walls are often old marks and may be treated with a proprietary damp sealant or an oil-based paint. This should be applied by brush, and it is recommended that the manufacturer's instructions are followed regarding drying times.

However, if the area of wall is still damp following treatment do not continue to decorate but bring in a damp specialist to look at the wall, as the problem might be coming either from the outside or from a water source in another house or flat.

Preparation for hanging

Once the room has been measured, and the walls stripped, filled, sealed and lined, it is then important to take time to check that all the tools and equipment you will need are in place before starting to hang the paper.

This includes knowing exactly where the first drop of wallpaper is going to be hung, probably over either the fireplace or the window (see page 15), and also checking that you know where to turn off the electricity when papering around light fittings (see pages 32–3). Thinking ahead at this stage will help to predict any likely problem areas, and will save time during the papering process.

Ensure that you have all the equipment you will need to hand, checking against the list on the right. Also check that all the tools and materials are clean: that there isn't any old adhesive on brushes or in the bucket, the craft knife has plenty of disposable blades (it is worth having a small tin to keep the sharp blades in), there is a nearby source of warm water and a sponge and that the floor is well covered with newspaper or some other protective sheeting.

Prepare sufficient quantities of paste (see page 22), so as not to run out halfway through papering. Remember that not all wallpaper outlets are open on a Sunday. Each roll of wallpaper will also need to be checked (see page 21) before starting to cut each length.

Tools and materials

Bucket(s)
Craft knife and blades
Decorator's scissors
Paper/graph paper
Paperhanger's brush
Pasting brush
Pasting table
Pencil
Plumb line
Protection for floor
(newspaper or plastic sheeting)
Rubbish bags for offcuts
Seam rollers
Spirit level
Sponge(s)
Stepladder
Straightedge (metal)
Tape measure (steel)
Wallpaper
Wallpaper paste

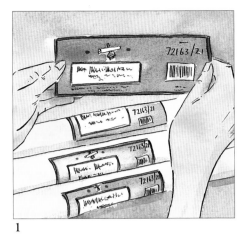

1

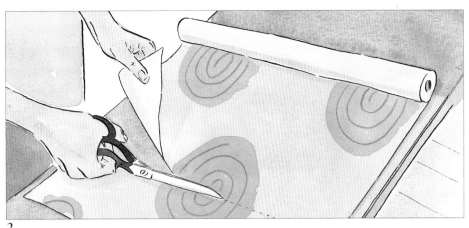

2

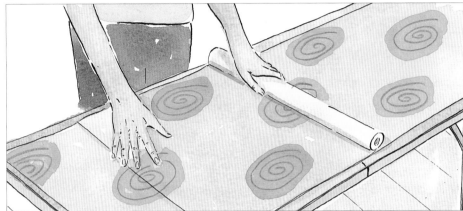

3

4

PREPARING WALLPAPER

It is better to double check all the rolls of wallpaper that you are planning to use before hanging the first length. This will help you check not only that you have the right amount and are not going to run out halfway through the job, but will also anticipate any problems with colour and design. Always check the wallpaper for possible faults before starting to cut and hang. Do this in daytime as they may not show up in artificial light.

1 Take all the wallpaper rolls that you are planning to use, and check before even opening them that they are all the same design number, and most importantly, have the same batch number (see pages 12–13.). Open the first wallpaper roll, remembering to keep the label.

2 Unroll the first roll of wallpaper on the pasting table, keeping the design side uppermost. Now measure the first piece of wallpaper to the required length and cut with the decorator's scissors.

3 If the paper has a pattern, place the second length on top of the first when unrolling it on the table, taking care to match the design (see page 15 for details on patterned wallpapers).

4 It is a good idea to mark T (for top) and B (for bottom) on the back of each length of patterned wallpaper with a pencil. This means that, even if you are cutting several lengths of paper at the same time, it will still be clear which way up the paper should be hung. When cutting, remember to allow the extra length at each end, as described on page 24, for trimming purposes.

Making your mark

It was once the custom to mark the name and address of the paper hanger, the make or origin of the paper and the date of decorating on the bare plaster wall before wallpapering. Why not keep up this tradition for future generations to find?

PREPARING PASTE

When the wallpaper has been cut into the required number of pieces, prepare the wallpaper paste. Always follow the manufacturer's recommendations for the type of paste to be used with the wallpaper that you have chosen. The various types of paste available are described on page 12.

If mixing your own paste, first make sure that you have the necessary equipment to hand. Following the quantities specified on the packet, measure the correct amount of water into the bucket. Then sprinkle the paste into the water, stirring to ensure that it is evenly distributed.

When all the paste has been added to the water, stir thoroughly. Let it stand for the required time, usually two or three minutes, then stir again. The paste should now be ready to use.

PASTING

Place a length of paper on the pasting table with the design facing down, making sure that the paper slightly overlaps both along the nearest edge of the table and at one end; this will stop any paste getting on to the face of the wallpaper. If this does happen, wipe any paste off with damp sponge.

1 Take the pasting brush and apply the adhesive to the back of the wallpaper, spreading it evenly all over, but not on the area 30cm (12in) away from the far edge of the table.

2 Now move the paper over to the other side of the table, again with the edge of the paper overlapping the table, and apply adhesive to the uncovered area with the pasting brush.

3 Fold the pasted paper over on itself about two-thirds of the way down and move the remaining wallpaper

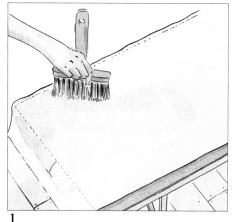

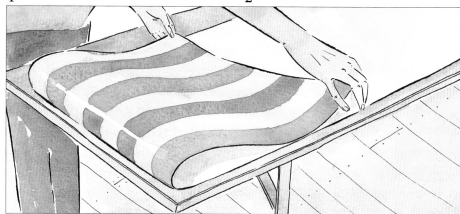

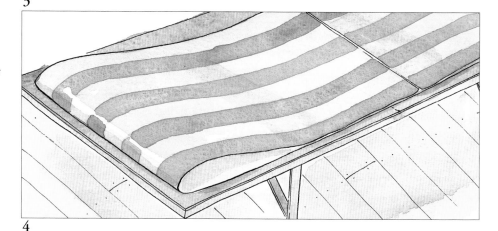

along the table. Cover the remaining paper in the same way as above, until the entire length is covered with paste.

4 Fold the bottom length of paper, again on to itself, and place so that it is almost touching the top fold. Please note that, providing the instructions about soaking time are followed carefully, there will be no problems of the paper sticking to itself.

Pasting made easy

If the adhesive has been mixed in a plastic bucket, tie a piece of string tautly across the top of the bucket. This will allow the pasting brush to be placed over the top of the bucket, without it actually falling in and getting the handle covered with paste.

SOAKING

All wallpaper must be left after pasting for a certain amount of time to allow the wallpaper paste to soak in.

It is most important to get this right. Soak your paper for too long and it will become much harder to hang; soak it too little and it may curl up and even shrink. The time allowed for soaking gives the paper time to expand and become more pliable – vital for that perfect finish. This time also means that the paper is less likely to create bubbles when it dries.

Every wallpaper roll has a label which should have precise instructions of how long to soak it for. To save time, it is possible to paste your second length of wallpaper while the first length is soaking. Take care not to let the two lengths get stuck together!

Clean pasting

When pasting the wallpaper take care not to get any paste on either the decorated face of the paper as it will stain, or on the pasting table. As an extra precaution, wipe the top of the table with a clean, damp sponge between pasting each length.

READY-PASTED WALLPAPER

There are a number of wallpapers available, usually vinyl coated, which have a water-activated adhesive on the back. The paper is measured and cut in the standard way, as described on page 21. Ready-pasted papers are usually sold with a tray. Half-fill the tray with water and place it at the base of the wall. It is a good idea to place a plastic sheet under the tray to stop any water getting on to the floorboards.

1 Loosely roll up the first length of wallpaper, with the design facing inwards. Place the roll in the tray, pasted side down, with the pasted side facing away from you towards the wall. Immerse for the recommended time, then hang the length as normal. When the edges of each length of vinyl paper have been joined together, smooth the joints and wipe down with a sponge, and roll down the edges with a plastic or wooden seam roller.

2 Sometimes these papers may have an excess of paste, which will show at the edges – just wipe away any excess paste with a sponge. If left to dry, the paste will leave marks on the surface of the wallpaper.

1

2

Hanging wallpaper

When the walls have been prepared and lined, and your chosen wallpaper cut and pasted, you should be ready to hang the first drop.

HANGING A STRAIGHT DROP

It is worth taking your time at this stage in order to ensure that the paper is hung accurately and that it is level. The instructions here explain how to hang a straight drop, here from the ceiling to the floor. This technique can then be adapted as necessary, for example for hanging the first drop over the fireplace, as recommended.

1 Before starting to hang the first drop, plumb and draw a vertical line from the ceiling or cornice to the skirting board (see page 14). To use a plumb line, place a small nail just below the ceiling or cornice and hang the plumb line from this. Mark the wall with a pencil at points along the length of the plumb line.

2 Join up the points on the wall using a straightedge and a pencil, to create a straight line that will act as the guiding line against which to place the edge of the first drop.

3 Take the first length of wallpaper, already pasted and left to soak (see pages 22–3), and with one hand, hold the top section of the paper up against the wall, lining the left edge up with the vertical line drawn on the wall. Hold the folds of paper with the other hand. If it is a very high room, it might be helpful to have someone there to hold the bottom of the length of paper while the top part is being put in place; this should help to prevent the paper tearing or stretching. The top of the length of wallpaper should be placed at the junction of the wall and the ceiling or cornice, with a 5cm (2in) overlap at the top for trimming purposes.

4 Having lined up the wallpaper with the pencil line on the wall, smooth it gently but firmly into position using the paperhanger's brush.

5 Work downwards, brushing the paper from the top to the bottom to remove any bubbles or creases. Leave

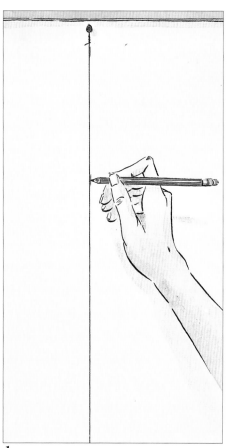

1

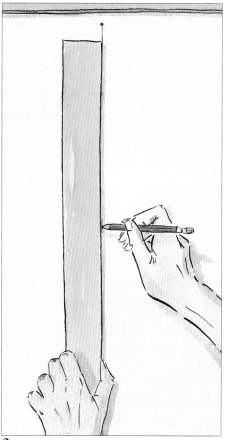

2

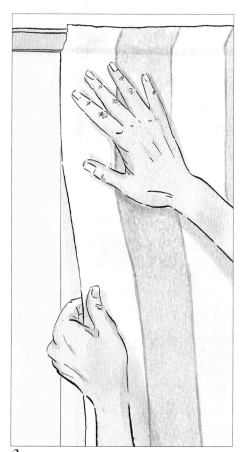

3

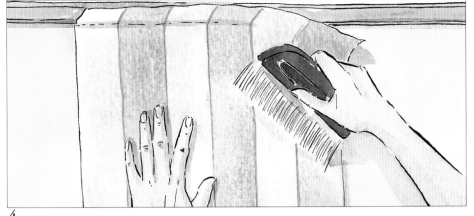

The right equipment

Always make sure that the plumb line is long enough, going right down to the skirting board. It is vitally important to get a really accurate line from ceiling to floor. Likewise, ensure that you are using decorators' scissors, and not the standard kitchen variety, when creasing and cutting.

4

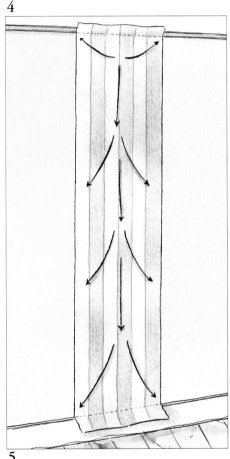

5

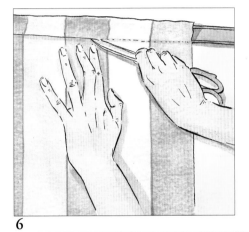

6

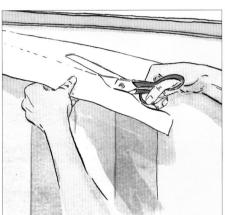

7

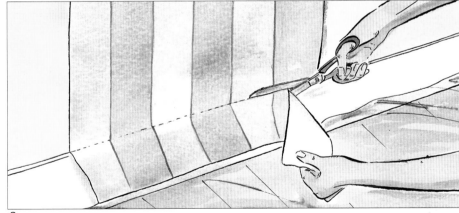

8

the bottom end of the paper loose, resting on the skirting board, and go back to the top.

6 Run the rounded blunt edge of the decorator's scissors slowly and gently across the line on the paper between the wall and the ceiling or cornice. This will emphasize the crease in the paper and will create a clear guideline for the final, accurate trim.

7 Gently pull the wallpaper away from the wall at the top and cut along the marked crease with the scissors. If you prefer to cut using a craft knife, leave the paper in place on the wall and run the knife along the crease. If the craft knife used is the type with a break-off, disposable blade, use one blade per cut. After cutting, push the paper back into place with the paperhanger's brush.

8 Now return to the paper at the bottom of the wall. Trim the overlap here by repeating the process described in the previous step. Again, if cutting the paper with a craft knife use new blade to ensure a clean, accurate cut. Push the paper firmly back on the wall with the brush. Finally, wipe off any wallpaper paste which may have been left on the ceiling or cornice and skirting board with a damp sponge.

HANGING THE SECOND LENGTH

The second length of paper should be cut, pasted and soaked for the correct amount of time. It is possible to leave the second length to soak while hanging the first.

1 Place the second length on the wall, matching the pattern, if any, to the first drop. If the pattern requires, you may need to allow extra at the top and bottom for trimming. Butt the second piece up against the first to form a tight join. Adjust if necessary to match with the pattern on the first drop.

2 Keep the bottom part folded while securing the top of this drop in place. Then repeat steps three to eight of hanging the first drop to paste and trim. Ensure that the pattern matches from ceiling to floor.

1

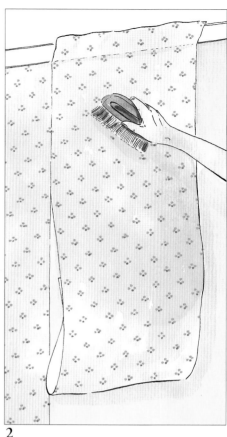

2

HANGING WALLPAPER AROUND A SINGLE EXTERNAL CORNER

1 When approaching an external corner, hang the nearest drop as described above. Paste and hang the corner piece so that an overlap of paper wraps smoothly round the corner.

2 Paste the next piece, hanging it so that it overlaps the previous drop, and aligns with the line of the wall at the corner, as depicted below. Trim the paper at the bottom and top as described on pages 24–5. If you are using a vinyl wallpaper you will need a special vinyl adhesive so that the paper sticks to itself on the overlap.

Helping hands

If papering a very high room or a staircase with a long drop, it is often helpful to have someone to hold the ladder and to help guide the wallpaper on to the lower part of the wall.

1

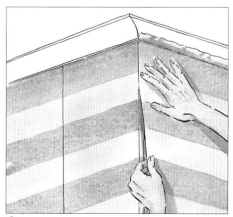

2

HANGING WALLPAPER AROUND A SINGLE INTERNAL CORNER

1 Having hung the paper from the fireplace or window, a corner is likely to be the next obstacle you will encounter. Measure the distance from the last length to the corner in three places: top, middle, and bottom. Add 2.5cm (1in) to the widest measurement and cut a length of paper to that width.

2 Paste, hang and join the next length to the drop already on the wall and, using the paperhanger's brush, smooth the paper into and around the corner on to the next wall.

3 There is sometimes a chance that the paper might crease while going round the corner; if so make a few small horizontal cuts in the paper with the scissors which will allow the creases to flatten out on the wall.

4 If the first drop of paper used has had to be cut to fit into the corner, you will be left with a strip of paper of varying width. This offcut should be used as the next length, hung into the corner on the adjacent wall. Measure the width of the offcut, then plumb and draw a line at this distance from the corner. Paste and hang this second drop, brushing the paper back into the corner. This drop should overlap the second drop to sit flush in the corner.

Luxurious look

Wallpapers have been designed to copy the types of wallcoverings that might be prohibitively expensive if using the real thing. Silk, moire and damask effect wallpapers are all available from specialist wallpaper suppliers at a fraction of the cost of the original (see pages 8–11 and 34–5).

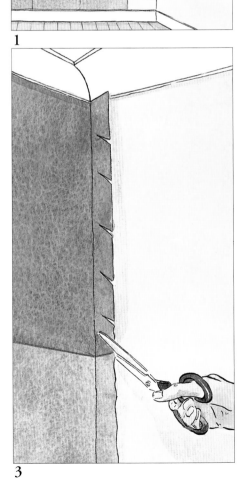

1

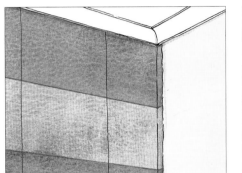

2

3

4

TRIMMING AROUND A FIREPLACE

1 On reaching the edge of the fireplace, hang the paper down and over the shelf, but only brush down to about 30cm (12in) above the fireplace.

2 Place a finger on the edge of the mantelpiece. With the other hand, use the paperhanger's brush to push the paper into the corner between the back of the fireplace and the wall.

3 Take the craft knife and cut horizontally along the middle of the shelf. Now brush down the paper above the fireplace into the back of the mantelpiece, cut and trim.

4 Push the paper underneath the shelf into place with the brush, and trim carefully around any fireplace mouldings. Finish off by trimming down the edge to the skirting board.

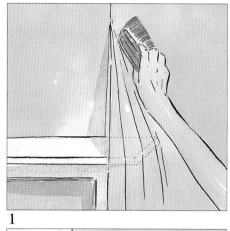

1

2

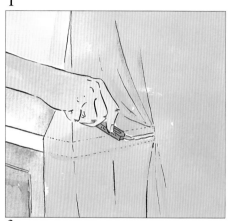

3

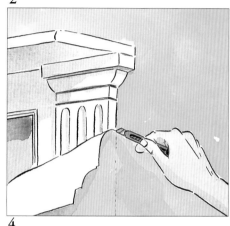

4

RADIATORS

1 The best way of papering around a radiator is to remove it completely. However, if this is not possible measure and hang a full length of paper. Brush down the top half only, allowing the bottom end to fall loosely.

2 Carefully pull the bottom half of the paper away from the wall and trim to fit behind the radiator, keeping as long as possible. Make two creases or marks in the paper to show where the brackets are. Cut upwards through the paper to these marks and make two small cuts, each in the shape of a 'v'.

3 Finally, brush the paper down behind the radiator, using a long-handled brush or roller. Repeat this process with as many drops of paper as are needed to hang behind the radiator. To ensure a clean finish, wipe away any excess paste from the front of the radiator with a damp sponge.

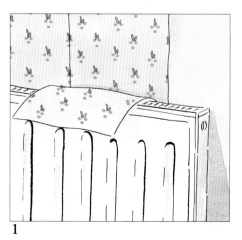

1

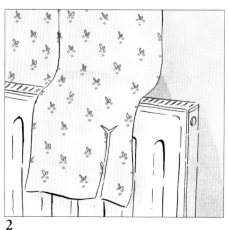

2

3

WINDOWS

If there is no fireplace in a room, then it is advisable to start papering at a window (see page 14), then to work away from the light around the room. For details of how to hang paper around a window without a recess, see below. If the window is wide enough, hang one drop centrally over the top of the window. If not, then drop a plumb line to the right of the window, some 12cm (4–5in) less than the width of the wallpaper so that the first drop of paper overhangs the window frame.

1 Paste and hang the first drop so that it is hanging loosely over one edge of the window frame. Trim the excess paper to the architrave or edge.

2 Brush the paper down into the architrave and then trim above and below the window.

1

1

2

RECESSED WINDOWS

1 Hang a length of paper over the window allowing enough paper to turn into and cover the depth of the recess, plus an extra amount for trimming down the window frame. Using the craft knife, make two cuts to the corners of the recess. Turn the paper into the recess and trim to the window frame, but do not brush down.

2 Next measure, cut and paste a short drop of paper which will cover the top of the recess or reveal (a), with extra paper to fold down the side of the recess (b) and fold up on to the main wall (c). Peel back the long drop to hang this piece in place.

3 Brush the long drop back in place and push up to the window frame with the brush. Trim into the side of the recess using the craft knife.

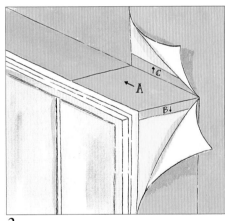

2

3

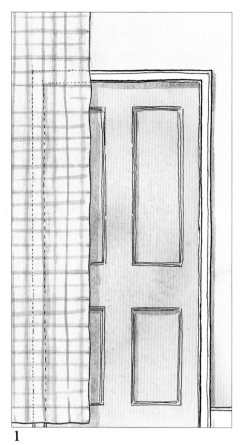

1

2

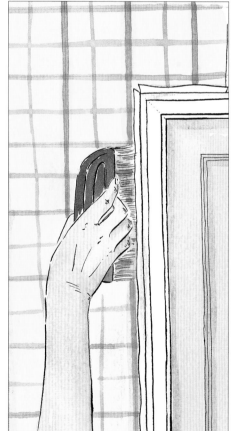

3

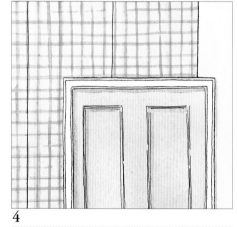

4

Doors

1 Hang the last full drop of wallpaper up to, but not over, the door. Paste the next length, but not the area that will be cut to allow for the door. Hang, allowing the paper to hang loosely over the door. Cut the paper, leaving a 5cm (2in) overlap around the door frame.

2 Press down on the top corner of the door frame to make an indentation in the paper. Using the decorator's scissors, cut diagonally from the edge of the paper at 45 degrees to this point.

3 Brush the paper into the angle between the wall and door frame. Trim the paper around the door frame with the craft knife.

4 Hang a short drop down to the top of the door frame then repeat this process on the other side of the door.

Decorative doorways

Doorways are often overlooked when a room is being decorated, but wallpaper can make a door into an attractive feature. Borders are easy to apply (see pages 36–7) and effective. It is also possible to paper the door itself – see the decorated moulded panels in the project on pages 68–71.

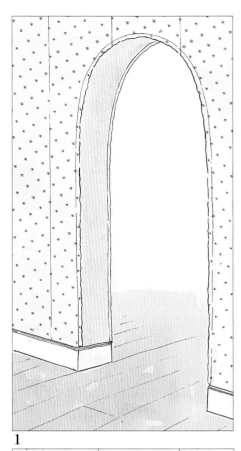

1

2

Sharp cutting

A craft knife with disposable blades is an important tool, especially when trimming paper around a door or window or other obstacle, as well as into the cornice and skirting board. The more blades used the better, to ensure a clean cut every time.

PAPERING AN ARCH BETWEEN TWO ROOMS

1 Paper the walls on either side and above the arch, allowing an extra 5cm (2in) overlap of paper around the edges.

2 Take this overlap round the corner into the arch by cutting several horizontal cuts in the edge of the paper.

If paper is being hung on the other side of the arch as well, repeat this process.

3 Cut a long strip of wallpaper just very slightly narrower than the width of the arch recess. Paste, fold and hang from the bottom, as in the picture below, taking the paper slowly up and around the inside of the recess and down the other side.

3

PAPERING AN ARCH WITH A RECESS

1 First paper the wall within the recess, allowing an extra amount of paper to overlap 5cm (2in) on to the back wall of the recess. Then follow steps two and three above to paper the inside of the arch. If the paper has a repeated vertical pattern, cut two strips of paper, which join and overlap at the top of the recess. Cut through both papers and peel back to remove the overlap.

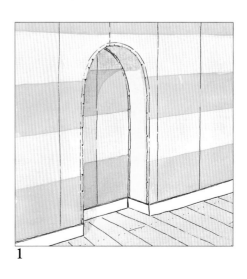

1

1

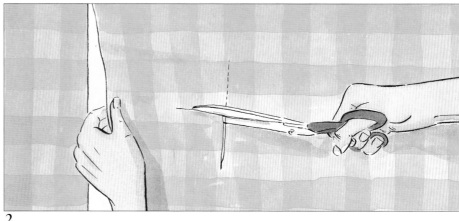

2

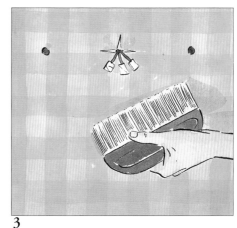

3

Wall fittings

Before tackling light fittings, always turn off the electricity. Remember that you will need to work during daylight hours.

1 First remove the light fitting from the wall and put to one side. Cover the exposed wires with electrical insulating tape. Replace the screws from the light fitting.

2 Hang the paper over the wires and screws, marking where the wires come out of the wall on the wallpaper with a pencil. With scissors or a craft knife make a very small cut in the paper, and bring the wires through, threading them from the back.

3 Brush the paper carefully on to the screws and smooth down. Let the paper dry before replacing the fitting.

Ceiling light

1 When papering the ceiling, paste and brush the length of paper up to the light fitting. Hold the paper over the light fitting, indenting the paper slightly with your finger to mark the centre of the light fitting.

2 Support the paper beyond the light fitting with one hand, and use a pair of scissors to cut through the paper at the marked point. Cut a cross in the paper large enough to gently pull the light fitting through, then paste the paper across to cover the rest of the ceiling.

3 Make small cuts in the paper around the light fitting, pushing the paper up to the ceiling and pushing it into the angle between the ceiling and the light fitting. Trim off the excess flaps of paper carefully with a craft knife, and wipe off any excess paste from the light.

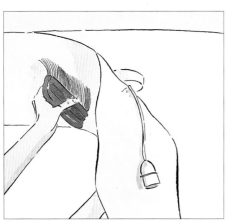

1

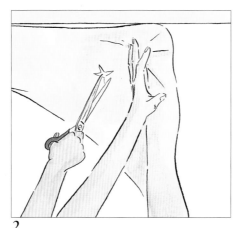

2

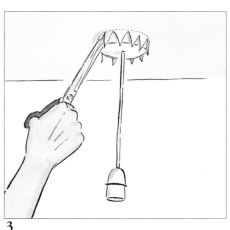

3

LIGHT SWITCHES

Turn off the electricity before starting to paper around any light switches or electrical sockets.

1 For best results, unscrew the switch plate but do not remove totally. Cut the paper so that about a 1cm (¹/₂in) overlap will slip behind the plate. Smooth the paper behind the plate, then replace and tighten the screws.

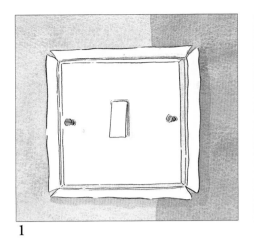

1

Safety first

Make sure that there is some electrical insulating tape available to cover exposed wires when wall fittings and light switches are being removed. If preferred use plastic block terminals instead. Do always double check that the electricity is turned off by switching on an overhead light.

FIXED SWITCH PLATES

1 If it is not possible to unscrew the switch plate then there is an alternative. Hang the paper so it falls loosely over the plate. Brush the paper down, allowing the switch beneath to make an impression in the paper.

2 Hold the paper firmly in place over the plate, and use a sharp craft knife to make four diagonal cuts from the middle of the plate to each corner. Carefully fold back the paper to the edges of the switch, pushing it into the angle between the wall and the switch plate with a decorator's brush.

3 Now trim the paper around the plate with a sharp craft knife making sure that the paper is cut tight up against it. This is a good time to think about replacing light switches, which can get dirty and scratched with constant use. Alternatively, paint the switch plate to match the wallpaper.

1

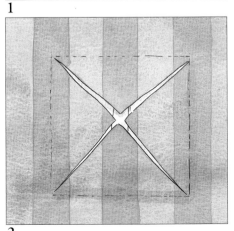

2

3

Special techniques
Different wall coverings

There are many different types of wallpaper and wallcoverings available other than those mentioned in this book so far. For a quick definition, all wallpapers, whether standard, vinyl or relief, which are 52cm (21in) wide, are known as a wallpaper. Anything wider, up to 140cm (55in) wide, is known as a wallcovering.

RELIEF PAPERS

The most commonly used relief papers are anaglypta and woodchip. Both these types of paper are ideal for use on uneven walls and rough surfaces, as they will cover up most imperfections. However, the wall does still need to be prepared properly before hanging these types of paper.

Anaglypta is easy to use as it is a lightweight paper, but it is very hard-wearing. Made from cotton and paper pulp, it is embossed when wet, which means that it keeps its texture when hung on the wall.

To hang relief papers, first prepare and line the walls as described on pages 16–9, then cut and paste the paper. Relief papers require a longer soaking time than standard wallpapers; always follow the instructions on the label.

1 Hang relief papers in the same way as standard paper (see pages 24–5), but take care not to roll down too hard on the paper as this could flatten the pattern. These types of paper are often painted over (see pages 60–3), so it is not always such a problem if the butt joints are not perfect as the paint will fill any small gaps.

2 Brush the paper into place, making sure that the edges are smoothed down properly against the wall.

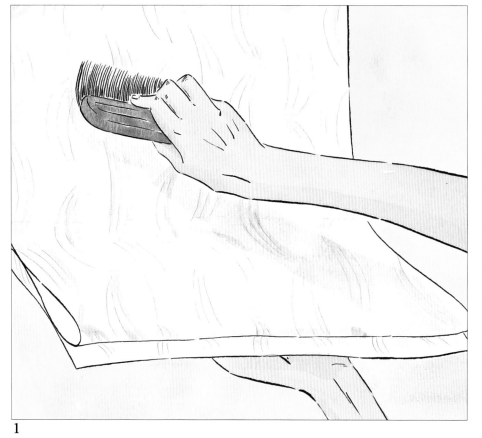

1

2

WALLCOVERINGS

There are many different types of wallcovering available, as listed below.

HESSIANS
Hessian was popular in the 1970s, and is now coming back into fashion.

GRASS CLOTH
Grass cloth is a natural product. The joins will show when hung.

FELTS
Felt is available paper-backed. Do not get any paste on the front of the felt.

FOILS
Most often available in gold or silver. Take care when hanging foils.

WIDE WIDTH VINYLS
Hard wearing, wide width vinyls are produced for use in public areas.

SILKS
A natural product, silks look beautiful and are very long lasting.

1 The main difference when hanging wallcoverings rather than wallpapers, is that it is the wall which is pasted first. Some wallcoverings will also require a coat of adhesive on the back to make them more supple and easier to work with. Always follow the manufacturer's instructions.

2 When joining the edges together, overlap by about 5cm (2in).

3 Cut through the overlapping wallcoverings with a very sharp craft knife and using a metal straightedge.

4 Take back the two edges of the wallcovering and remove the strip of paper underneath. Finish by brushing the wallcovering back onto the wall and rolling down the edges.

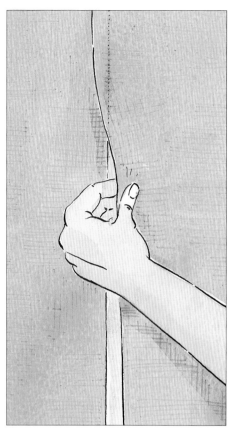

1

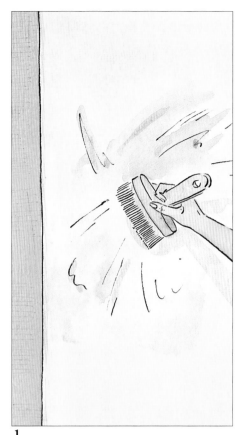

2

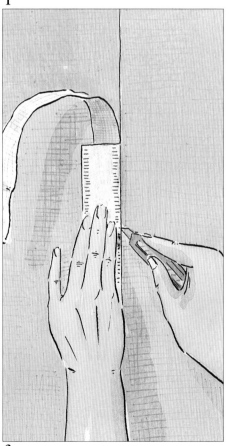

3

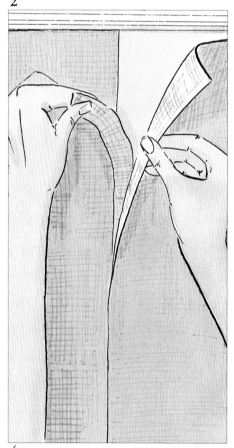

4

Hanging borders and friezes

Borders and friezes can brighten up a whole house or room, with very little expense and effort. Although traditionally hung beneath the ceiling or cornice, both can work well if hung at any height around the room.

HANGING BORDERS

1 There are a huge range of styles and colours of borders available. Choose a border to complement the colour of the wall, and plan the desired effect before starting to hang the border.

2 To hang the border along the top of a wall, measure down from the ceiling or cornice to where the bottom of the border will be (if you wish to create a dado effect then measure from the skirting board upwards). Using a spirit level and a straight-edge, mark a pencil line at this height horizontally around the room. Measure the length of the first wall, adding a 5cm (2in) overlap. Cut the first strip of border to this length.

3 To avoid getting adhesive all over your pasting table, place a length of lining paper on the table, underneath the frieze or border, before pasting. Borders can be applied to wallpaper or to a painted surface. For best results use the type of adhesive recommended by the manufacturer.

4 Starting from one corner, apply the border to the wall, making sure that the pencil guideline is covered.

5 Continue applying the border to the wall, using a brush or sponge to secure it in place.

6 When applying the second length of border to the wall, overlap the first at the corner.

7 Cut into both strips of border in the corner with a craft knife and remove the top overlap.

8 Peel back both ends of border from the corner and remove the small strip of paper underneath. Place the two ends back together on the wall and roll then sponge down the joins.

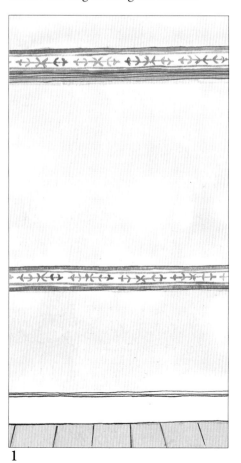

1

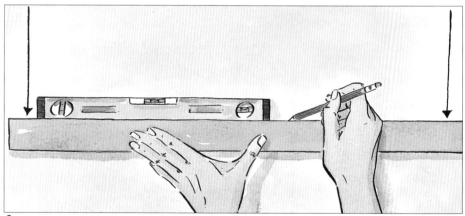

2

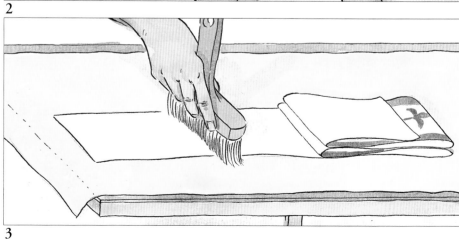

3

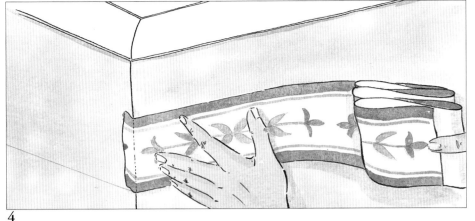

4

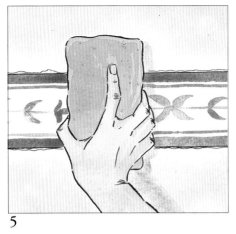

5

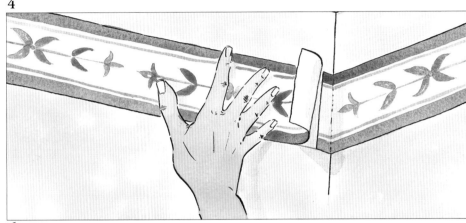

6

7

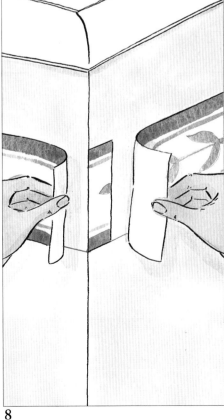

8

HANGING FRIEZES

Friezes are wider, and often more elaborate, than borders. Usually hung either above or below an existing picture or dado rail, they may be used instead of these features if neither exist in the room, and can look effective running up the wall parallel to the stairs. Friezes can also be hung on the ceiling (see pages 60–3).

When hanging friezes over a wallpaper use a standard adhesive, but if the wallpaper has a vinyl surface you will need to use a ready-mixed tub paste (see page 13 for details), or a specialist frieze adhesive.

Measure, cut and paste the frieze as described in steps two to eight above. It is possible to create the effect of a frieze by either using a whole strip of wallpaper hung horizontally, or by using several rows of borders together.

Buy generously

Remember to take the dimensions of the area to be decorated, i.e. the distance around the walls and the height, when buying wallpaper. It is always worth buying an extra roll, just in case the paper on the wall gets damaged at some stage in the future.

HANGING BORDERS AROUND WINDOWS AND DOORS

Borders can be used on plain wallpaper, or even on painted surfaces (follow the manufacturer's instructions for the most appropriate type of adhesive to use). They can be used to great effect around doors and windows, making an interesting and unusual feature out of these areas.

1 Using a spirit level and straightedge, mark out horizontal lines with a pencil around the window equal to the width of the border being used. Then measure the height and width of the door or window.

2 Following these measurements, cut the border into four lengths for a window (three for a door), adding an extra 5cm (2in) to each length for trimming. Paste and hang the first strip of border along the top of the window, making sure that the extra length is equal at both ends.

3 Hang the border down both sides and underneath the window (down the two sides for a door).

4 Take a craft knife and steel ruler and make a diagonal cut in the overlapping ends of the borders from the exterior to the interior corner.

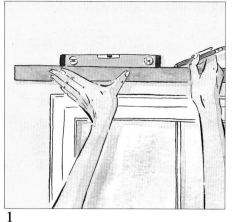

1

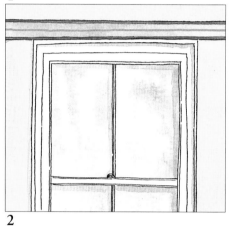

2

3

5 Remove the resulting offcut from the top, then carefully pull away both ends of the border from the wall in order to remove the small offcut of paper from underneath.

6 Replace the ends of the border, smoothing down and pressing the join with a seam roller. Repeat in all four corners, then sponge down the border to remove any excess adhesive.

Forward planning

Make a simple scale drawing on a piece of graph paper if it is difficult to visualize what he finished effect will be. Also, take note of the width of the border in question, making sure that it is in proportion to the window or door being decorated.

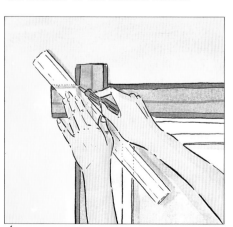

4

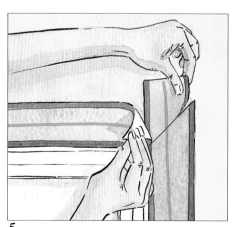

5

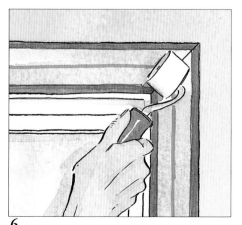

6

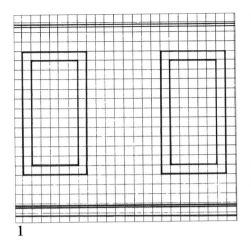

1

CREATING PANELS ON WALLS AND DOORS

This is a simple but effective way of using borders. See pages 56–9 for further details on set on designs.

1 First make a scale drawing on a sheet of paper of the exact area and design required. This is most important as it will help you to plan the design.

2 Plumb a line on the wall in what will be the centre of the panel, then mark the wall at the top of the panel.

3 Make a horizontal line at this point with a spirit level and straightedge, to the width required.

4 Next plumb down from both ends of this line to what will be the bottom edge of the panel. Mark the bottom line on the wall. Measure, paste and hang the border, following the steps described opposite.

5 Finish by cutting and trimming the four corners using a craft knife and straightedge. As with the border round the window, make a diagonal cut from the exterior to interior corner. Pull back both ends at each corner, remove the cut piece from underneath, then place the paper back on the wall before rolling and sponging down the edges.

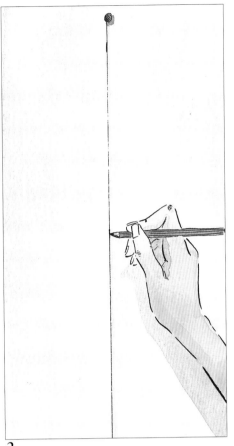

2

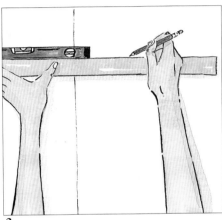

3

Border crazy

Panels created with wallpaper borders can be applied around mirrors on the wall, or even around a favourite poster or picture. Not only are borders inexpensive, but they are also easy to paste and hang and are available in a huge variety of designs and colours.

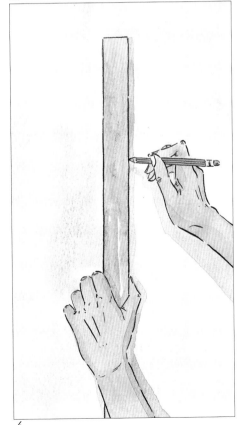

4

5

Trouble shooting and repairs

Help line

All wallpaper manufacturers have a technical department; do not be afraid to contact them, either directly or through the supplier.

General problems

This section gives advice on avoiding some of the common problems and faults which may occur when working with wallpaper.

Even the most professional paper hangers do, from time to time, come up against problems. Do not panic. Even if something appears to be going wrong, there is usually a simple remedy.

Check first that all the wallpaper that you are planning to use is perfect by opening all the rolls you will need, before starting to cut and paste, and inspecting them carefully.

If there is a printing error or fault running through them (a very rare occurrence), return them with their labels to the supplier as quickly as possible. The supplier will be able to order some more rolls of the same paper, but from a different batch.

If, however, there is a tear, misprint or mark on just one roll, keep the roll and its label. It might be possible to use the rest of the roll, but it is best to call the supplier to explain the situation.

Do remember that it will be difficult for any supplier to give a refund for damaged paper if the actual roll of paper and its label is not returned.

Creating a perfect finish

The following are some of the most common faults seen in wallpaper after it has been hung. Most of these problems can be avoided if the correct preparation procedures detailed on the preceding pages are followed.

DISCOLOURATION

Wallpaper may discolour if the walls have not been sealed properly (see pages 18–19) before hanging the paper, if there is paste on the front of the paper or if certain pigments in the paper have faded in excessive sunlight.

MOULD GROWTH

Occasionally patches of mould may grow on wallpaper. This could be due to a number of causes, such as damp walls or condensation, meaning that the paste will dry very slowly. Sometimes small patches of old size or paste remaining on the walls will also cause mould to appear – these should be cleaned off before papering the wall.

POOR MATCHING

If you have had difficulty matching the pattern on two drops of paper it is probably because of poor pasting. Under or over-soaking the length of paper reduces adhesion and makes the paper difficult to handle when you line up the pattern.

RUST SPOTS

Rust spots may appear on wallpaper that has been hung over unsealed steel pins in timber or wall boarding. Always mask or seal all old nail or pin marks on the wall before lining.

STAINING

Stains may appear if the walls are damp, if paste has been allowed to get on to the front of the paper or if the paper has been applied over an unsuitable or non-porous surface, for example tiles, plastic or gloss paint.

TEARING

If the paper tears easily when it is applied to the wall then it is likely that too much paste has been used, or even that the paste is too thin. As a result the paper is too wet and therefore difficult to handle. Careless handling or the use of blunt tools may also tear paper.

Trial run

Another advantage of lining the walls first is that many of these problems will show up on the lining paper, so the problem can be remedied before the actual wallpaper is applied.

WHITE SEAMS SHOWING

White seams may appear between two drops while the paper is drying out, especially if it has not been properly butted together when applied to the wall (see page 26), or if there is no lining paper underneath. Another reason for this might be that the paper has shrunk because it was not given enough time to soak after being pasted (see page 23). Also, a few of the darker types of wallpaper available have a white edge which may show. Some manufacturers provide a special felt pen just for this problem.

1

1 Take care when hanging one length of paper next to another, in order to avoid a white seam showing.

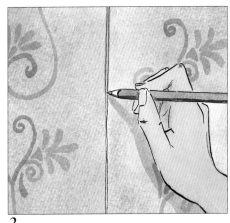

2

2 Use the pen supplied by the paper manufacturer, or a coloured crayon, to colour in the white seam.

BUBBLING

1 Bubbles may appear if too much paste has been applied to the paper. Sometimes the bubbles will disappear as the paper dries out.

2 However, if the bubbles remain, pierce each one with a craft knife to allow any excess paste to escape. Sometimes the bubbles are just full of air; again just pierce the paper with a knife to let the air out.

3 Wipe down each bubble with a damp sponge to remove any paste. If the bubbles were just full of air, then apply a little paste with a small artists' brush to aid adhesion, before sponging down to create a smooth finish.

1

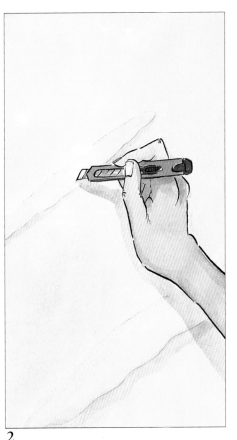

2

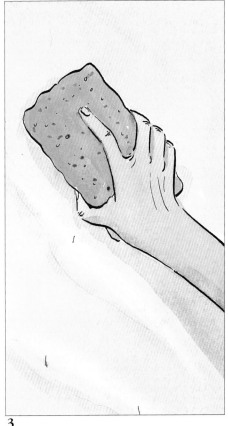

3

CREASES

Creases normally occur when the wallpaper is hung round a corner, either external and internal. As outlined on pages 26 and 27, when papering round a corner it is advisable to make a few small cuts in the overlapping paper in order to enable the paper to lie absolutely flat on the wall. If there are large creases showing through it is possibly because the overlap allowed for the corner was too large. With small creases, use a craft knife to let out excess paste or air, as described for bubbles on page 41.

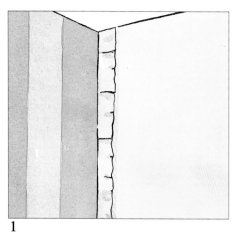

1

1 Measure carefully to ensure that the paper allowed to overlap the corner is no more than 2.5cm (1in) wide.

2

2 Cut small nicks in the overlap with the decorator's scissors to allow the paper to lie flat on the wall.

LIFTING SEAMS

1 Seams that do not stick to the wall are a common and highly irritating fault, which is nearly always caused by not lining the walls first.

2 If possible, carefully lift back the problem seams. Use a small artists' brush to apply some adhesive to the underside of the wallpaper. There is a special overlap adhesive available which would also be suitable for use here.

3 Roll the wallpaper back in place with a seam rolling tool, then wipe the seams with a sponge to remove any adhesive on the surface of the paper. If the paper has a raised pattern, do not press too hard with the rolling tool.

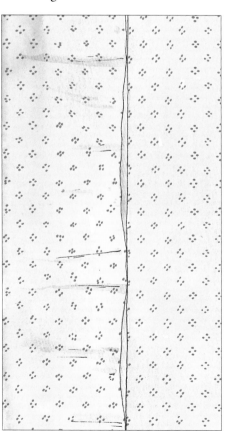

1

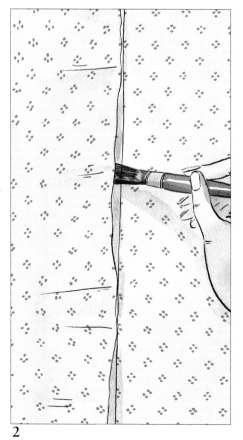

2

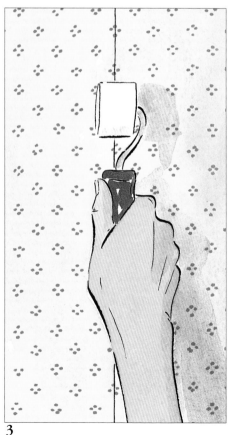

3

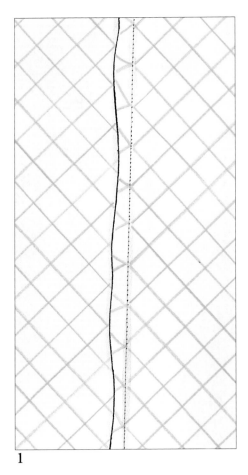

1

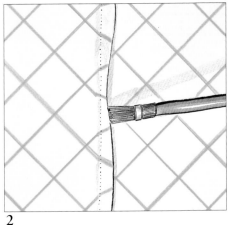

2

3

Overlapping

1 The drops of paper should butt up neatly against each other. But if an overlap does occur it may not stick, as pictured here. This is a problem that can be solved in a similar way to that of lifting seams (see page 42). Vinyl papers are particularly difficult. Try to avoid overlapping by always following the pencil guidelines on the wall.

2 To stick the paper, gently pull back the overlap. Apply an appropriate adhesive to the paper underneath the overlap with an artists' brush. Try to be careful not to get adhesive on any of the wallpaper that will show.

3 Wipe down the overlap with a damp sponge to remove any excess adhesive and then roll the paper securely in place with the seam roller.

Unstuck papers

1 Sometimes large areas of paper may peel off, as pictured here. This is often because without lining paper underneath the wallpaper, adhesive simply will not stick to the wall.

It may be that there is a residue of distemper on the wall. Remove the strip of paper from the wall and wash the wall thoroughly, removing all loose powder and flakes. Line the wall (see pages 18–19) and re-hang the paper.

A different kind of paste

One of the worst products for staining wallpaper is toothpaste. Always protect any wallpaper around a basin with glass or tiles.

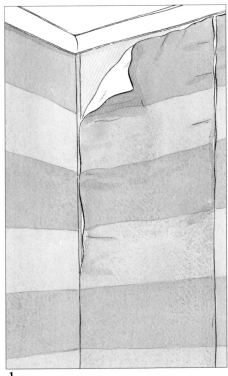

1

Preparation is the key

Most of the problems described here are caused by the same reason – bad substrate or poor preparation. The more time spent on the preparation, lining and sizing, the less chance there is of faults or problems occuring.

If there is any fault with the wallpaper contact the supplier immediately. The longer it is left, the more difficult it will be to reach a satisfactory conclusion.

If any of the problems described here persist, then the best solution is to strip off the affected lengths of paper and start again, ensuring that the wall is scrupulously prepared first.

Using two papers and hanging into a corner

Decorating one room with two different wallpapers, one placed above the other and separated by a dado rail or border, can add considerable interest to the walls. It is also a cost-effective way of using an expensive paper.

Planning your time

DAY ONE

AM: Prepare materials. Start wallpapering in clockwise direction

PM: Paper into and round corner

DAY TWO

AM: Continue papering in clockwise direction

PM: Take paper over and around the door frame

Tools and materials

Wallpaper

Decorator's scissors

Wallpaper paste

Pasting table

Pasting brush

Stepladder

Bucket

Paperhanger's brush

Tape measure

Craft knife and blades

Straightedge

Plumb line

Pencil

Combining two or more papers in a room is a technique that dates back to the earliest days of wallpaper. At that time it reflected the high cost of wallpaper, and the fact that the lower areas of walls normally suffered by far the most wear and tear – which remains in the modern home.

By using a different and cheaper or more durable paper for the lower area, usually beneath a dado rail, one can renew the paper on that area as often as necessary without having to redecorate the whole room. If there is

no dado rail, why not use a paper border to create the effect of a dado rail instead? There are hundreds of attractive borders on the market, including some that are even designed specifically to look like dados. Where there is a picture rail as well, you could also use a different design above that.

In this project we chose two complementary wallpapers in gentle hues of warm beige and pale blue. The textured surface and slightly distressed effect combined to create a Shaker or Scandinavian feel to the room. We completed the look by using a paper border beneath the cornice. The same border, although slightly narrower in width than that used on the walls, was used to decorate the small tray table and another part of the same roll was used to pick out the corners of the door panels.

Choosing designs and styles that co-ordinate in this way is rather like matching clothes. There are countless possibilities, and the governing factors are the room in question, your own taste and the style you wish to achieve.

Day One

Step 1

Start papering the room, working clockwise away from the fireplace or window. If using two papers, start with the upper section, from the cornice to the dado rail. When this is complete then hang the lower level, working from the dado rail to the skirting board. Cut and trim each section as if papering a full length wall (see pages 24–5).

When approaching the first corner of the room, measure the distance from the edge of the last drop of wallpaper to the corner in three places, at the top, middle, and bottom (see page 27).

Step 2

Take the longest of the three measurements and cut the next piece of wallpaper to this width. Cut the paper on the pasting table, using a craft knife and straightedge to make an accurate line. Reserve the offcut. Paste and hang this length from the cornice, brushing the resulting small overlap of paper into and around the corner onto the adjacent wall with the paperhanger's brush.

Step 3

Measure the width of the offcut. Plumb a line at this distance from the corner, and mark at various intervals down the wall using a pencil. Join up these marks to draw a vertical line on the wall.

Step 4

Hang the offcut of paper on this line, pushing the paper back into the corner and over the overlap using the paperhanger's brush. Continue hanging paper in a clockwise direction from here on. For details on hanging paper round an external corner, see page 26.

1

2

3

4

Optical illusions

Striped wallpaper will add height and elegance to any room. There are a huge range of vertically striped wallpapers available, from those with pale, fresh colours to much richer and heavier colour combinations. Horizontal stripes are less traditional, but have the power to open up small spaces.

5

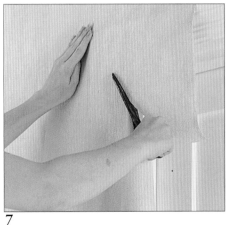

6

7

8

9

Day Two

Step 5

When you reach the door, hang the first length of paper that will overlap the door frame, allowing it to hang loosely over the door. When pasting this length, it is easiest not to paste the section of paper that will be cut away. (See page 30 for more information on hanging paper around a door.)

Step 6

Press down into the corner of the door frame, indenting the paper to indicate where it should be trimmed.

Step 7

Roughly trim away the paper that is hanging over the door. Then use the decorator's scissors to cut from the edge of the paper at an angle of 45 degrees to the mark made in the paper at the corner of the door frame. Cut the paper to within a couple of centimetres (1in) from the door frame. This will be trimmed later.

Step 8

Brush the paper firmly into the angle between the wall and the door frame using the paperhanger's brush.

Step 9

Trim the paper by cutting into the door frame with a craft knife. If the door is wide enough, hang one short length to fall to the top of the door frame, then repeat this process on the right-hand side of the door.

Finally, wipe off any paste from the surface of the door, before continuing to paper around the room.

Papering a staircase with sloping walls

Staircase areas really are no more difficult to paper than any other area. With a few expert tips and some careful preparation you will find it easy to achieve an impressive and polished finish.

Planning your time
....

DAY ONE

AM: Prepare walls and materials. Plumb a line and mark on wall

PM: Paste and hang the first two lengths. Trim at top and bottom

DAY TWO

AM: Hang paper on the return wall, working away from corner

PM: Continue hanging. When finished clear away tools and materials

Tools and materials
....

Wallpaper

Tape measure

Pencil

Plumb line

Straightedge (long)

Decorator's scissors

Stepladder

Masking tape

Wallpaper paste

Pasting table

Pasting brush

Bucket

Paperhanger's brush

Craft knife and blades

Straightedge (short)

S taircase areas also offer the opportunity to be adventurous, either through your choice of pattern or by using two or more papers. There are two main reasons for papering a staircase. One is that on stairs, even when there is a half-landing, there is seldom any furniture. This means that the walls provide the most scope for creating interest. Secondly, as one does not tend to linger on stairs and they are only seen in passing, it is possible to consider using a design that might be too bold for, say, a bedroom or living-room.

The only constraint when choosing wallpaper might be that stairs usually lead into halls and landings, so if you want to create a cohesive overall look you will need to think carefully about how to co-ordinate the decoration of the stairs with the adjoining areas.

Like any thoroughfare, stairs are subject to a lot of wear and tear. For this reason too, the use of two wallpapers, as in the previous project, may well be appropriate, especially if children are around. Felt-tip pens and sticky fingers have made a lot of staircase walls look old and tatty long before their time!

Do not be daunted by the challenge of papering a staircase, even if it has sloping walls. It may not be quite as straightforward as a simple room, and may involve a considerable height and the odd tricky corner, but if you follow the general principles of hanging paper, as described in the Basic techniques section on pages 24–5, you will find it no more difficult than any other project.

Day One

Step 1

When papering a staircase it is important to identify where the longest drop will be. This should be the first drop that you hang. Mark an accurate vertical line on the wall here, which will then act as a guideline for hanging further lengths. It is probable that at least one of the walls on a staircase will be sloping, increasing the need for an accurate vertical line to work from.

In this case, the widest point of the wall is at the bottom. Measure out from the corner at this point some 5cm (2in) less than the width of a standard roll of wallpaper (see page 34).

Step 2

Drop a plumb line from the top of the wall to the mark made in the previous step. Mark the wall with a pencil at intervals down the plumb line, then join up the marks with a straightedge to create a vertical guideline on the wall.

Step 3

Paste and hang the first length to the left of this line. This will act as a guide for lining up the wallpaper pattern when hanging the second drop into the sloping corner. Never use the wall itself as a guide, instead always refer back to the plumbed line. Trim the paper at the top with the craft knife.

Step 4

Hang the second drop, butting it up tightly and accurately against the previous drop. Remember that when using a patterned paper to allow the extra length for trimming purposes (see page 15). Use the paperhanger's brush to brush the paper into place.

Step 5

Continue brushing the paper downwards, smoothing it into and around the corner. If brushing the paper onto a sloping wall the overlap will be smallest at the bottom of the drop, where the wall is widest.

1

2

3

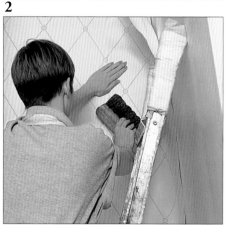

4

5

6

7

Step 6

Trim the paper at the bottom of this drop, using a short straightedge to push the paper into the angle of the skirting board and cutting it with a craft knife. Trim any excess paper from the overlap.

Day Two

Step 7

Hang the next length of paper on the return wall, working away from the corner. Trim the paper at the bottom of this drop with a craft knife, following the angle of the skirting board.

Safety is very important when hanging wallpaper on a staircase. Make sure that no paste is spilt on the stairs, and that the stepladder has suction pads on its legs to prevent it from slipping. It is also worth padding the top of the ladder, as seen in steps three and four, to stop it marking the wallpaper. This is easily done by wrapping masking tape around the top.

Hanging wallpaper horizontally

Try hanging lengths of wallpaper horizontally instead of vertically in a room and using alternately coloured designs to create an eye-catching and contemporary finish that is both different and fun.

Wallpapers, with the exception of friezes and borders, are generally intended to be hung vertically. However, some wallpapers look just as effective, and certainly more striking, when hung horizontally, and there is nothing to prevent you from using them in this way if you so wish.

There is one important point to remember. When hanging two papers vertically it is a positive advantage for one design to be stronger than the other, but when hung horizontally it is generally best to keep to the same plain design in different colourways. However, they can be applied either in an alternating or irregular order. If you want to be even more daring, cut out squares from papers of various colours and apply them to the wall – again either in a regular pattern or at random.

This project uses two plain papers in vibrant green and silver. The same basic principles of careful planning and preparation apply whether hanging paper horizontally or vertically. However, the lengths of paper will be less easy to manage on your own, and you will probably find it useful to have an extra pair of hands helping out. Start hanging from the second length down. This ensures that there will be one straight horizontal length which can be used as a guideline, even if the ceiling level is uneven.

When hanging paper horizontally, you can normally take lengths of paper around shallow corners, for example chimney breasts, without losing the alignment, but start a new length in each corner of the room.

Day One

Step 1

Prepare and line the walls. Note that if hanging wallpaper horizontally it is advisable to hang the lining paper vertically (see page 19) so the edges of the lining paper do not correspond with the edges of the wallpaper. From the cornice, measure down a distance of 2.5cm (1in) less than a standard roll of wallpaper (see page 34).

Step 2

Using a spirit level make pencil marks at this level around the room. Join up the marks with a straightedge to make a pencil line at this height on each wall.

Step 3

Make a second pencil mark 52cm (21in) below the first, which is the width of a standard roll of wallpaper.

Step 4

Take the spirit level and again mark at various intervals in pencil at this level around the room.

Step 5

Join up all the marks using a pencil and a metal straightedge to create a second horizontal line around the room.

1

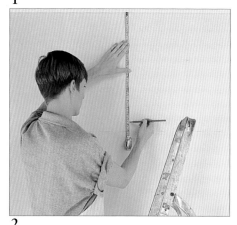

2

3

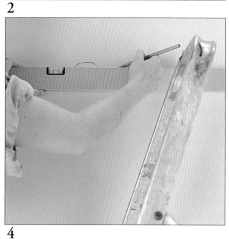

4

5

6

8

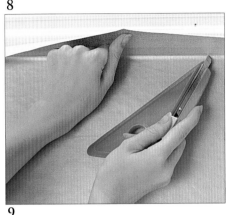

9

7

Day Two

Step 6
Paste and hang a strip of wallpaper between these two lines. Work from left to right and brush the paper into place using the decorator's brush. Ensure that the paper lines up accurately with the pencilled line.

Step 7
Hang a contrasting paper below the first strip, lining it up accurately with the first.

Step 8
Work down the wall, hanging alternate lengths of paper. The strip at the bottom may need to be cut to fit before pasting, allowing a 2.5cm (1in) overlap, which will then be trimmed into the skirting board.

Step 9
Finish off by hanging the length at the top, brushing it up into the cornice. Trim with the craft knife.

Creating a set on design in a hallway

Wallpaper borders can be used to achieve a number of striking architectural effects. Cut out simple strips from two different colours of wallpaper to create these stunning and dramatic three-dimensional effect panels.

Wallpaper borders are among some of the most useful items available to the interior decorator. Borders date back to the earliest days of wall coverings, when they were originally applied to conceal unsightly tacks and fixings. They will always be firm favourites with home decorators because they are easy to put up and immensely versatile. Borders are ideal for creating different styles, for balancing, emphasizing and linking areas, and for uniting diverse styles and furnishings. They can be

applied above a skirting board or below a cornice or picture rail. Alternatively, they can be used as a substitute for a dado or picture rail.

Borders can also be used 'set on' to plain wallpaper, as in this project, to create an elegant frame or panel effect. Some ready-made borders have co-ordinating corners, which greatly enhance a design as well as making the corners easier to finish. However, excellent results can also be obtained by simply using strips cut from contrasting coloured wallpapers.

Begin by papering the wall and then cutting out strips of contrasting wall-papers to create panels with a dramatic three-dimensional effect. The main requirement for this job is precision, both in planning the project, with a scale drawing, and in measuring the panels and making sure that they are completely straight and equidistant. The best way to achieve a high-quality result is to draw the design accurately on the wall first.

Day One

Step 1

Measure the wall that you are planning to decorate, then make a detailed scale drawing of the panels. Transfer the design onto the wall using a ruler and pencil.

When planning this project it is worth considering the direction from which any natural light falls on the wall. This will affect how the dark and pale edges of the panel should be placed. For further information on planning and creating set on designs, see page 39.

Step 2

Plumb a line from the ceiling or cornice in the centre of the wall. This will be the centre of the main, central panel.

Step 3

Measure 30cm (12in) down this line from the top. Make a small pencil point on the wall to mark what will be the height of the top of the panel.

Step 4

Draw a horizontal line at this level the same width as the finished panel. Use a spirit level and a steel straightedge to ensure that the top line of the panel is straight and level.

Step 5

Hang plumb lines down from both ends of the pencilled line to indicate where the sides of the panel will be. Make marks at regular intervals on the wall and join with a straightedge. Join these two lines at the bottom with a spirit level to mark the bottom of the panel.

1

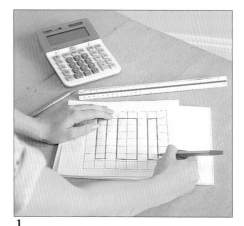

2

3

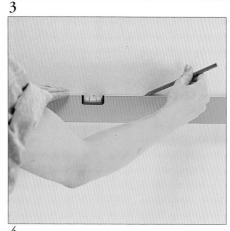

4

5

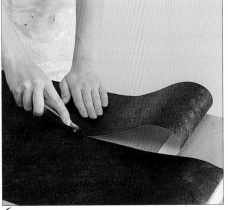

6

7

Step 6
Cut a long strip of the darker paper 8cm (3in) longer than the height of the panel.

Step 7
Place the wallpaper right side up on the pasting table. Butt up against the edge of the table. Mark 5cm (2in) in from the edge, then cut two strips of this width. Repeat the process with the paler paper.

Day Two

Step 8
Paste the two strips and allow them time to soak. Hang the outside left (vertical) strip first, along the guidelines marked on the wall, and smooth down with a sponge. Then hang the the outside bottom, or horizontal, strip.

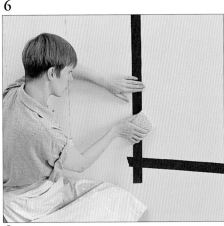

8

9

Step 9
Repeat this process on the other side of the panel but use two strips of the paler coloured wallpaper. Mitre the corner by holding a small straightedge at the angle where the two strips cross. Cut diagonally through both strips of paper with a craft knife. Lift up the ends of the two strips to remove the offcuts, then replace the strips on the wall and sponge down to secure.

Step 10
To finish the panel, cut four strips of paper, each 2.5cm (1in) wide. Cut two from the pale and two from the darker wallpaper. Apply them to the panel as contrasts to the wider strips, using the dark strips inside the pale, and vice versa. Take time to stand back and admire the dramatic effect that this creates before completing the two side panels in the same way.

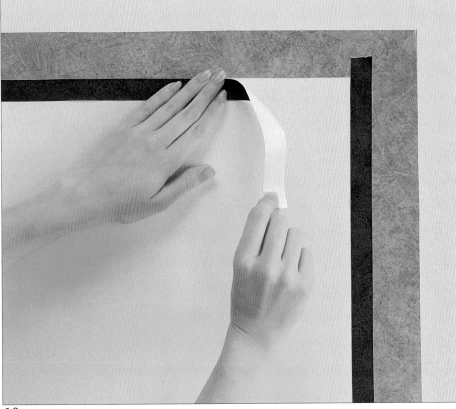

10

Papering a fireplace and hanging a frieze

As well as revealing a tried and tested method for papering around a fireplace, this project will show you how to use relief papers to create a stunning frieze. You will be surprised how easy it is to recreate this glamorous look!

Wallpaper will create a unified and decorative look in any room, but people are sometimes reluctant to tackle hanging paper around obstacles, such as fireplaces and windows. However difficult papering around these obstacles may appear, you will find that the simple and failsafe techniques described here can be easily followed for perfect results every time.

Relief papers, a name given to all wallpapers with a raised design, are available in a huge variety of designs and prices. Anaglypta and wood chip wallpapers have been extensively used in the last few decades, not only to create

texture on walls and ceilings, but also to cover a multitude of defects. This has given them a very bad image, which is a great shame because they can be used to great effect in any room. They are ideal for creating features in an otherwise plain room – hang them around a cornice or on the bottom half of a wall. They can even be used on ceilings, an area usually neglected in most homes.

There are so many different designs of frieze available, from timber tongue-and-groove effects through to art deco styles, that you are bound to find one that suits your taste. Alternatively, using colour to highlight the relief pattern of a frieze will enhance the design and create a special, personalized look. Gold and silver are especially effective – just rub a little gold paint into the raised design on the frieze for a really sumptuous feel.

Day One

Step 1

The shape of any fireplace is unique and, as when hanging round any obstacle that stands out from the wall, special care needs to be taken to trim the paper carefully into the angles of the fireplace. If working from one edge, hang a full drop of paper from the ceiling, allowing the lower section of paper to hang loosely over the fireplace.

Step 2

Brush and smooth the paper down until you reach the inside and outside edges of the mantelpiece. Make an indentation in the paper with your finger at this point.

Step 3

With a craft knife, cut horizontally along the middle of the mantelpiece shelf, using the indentation in the paper made in the previous step as a guideline.

Step 4

Brush the paper firmly down into the top of the mantelpiece. Using a craft knife, trim the paper carefully across the top.

Step 5

Then brush the paper into the side of the fireplace, using the craft knife to trim the paper accurately into the edges. Brush and trim the paper at the bottom of the drop into the skirting board. Paper around the rest of the fireplace using the same method. For further information on papering around a fireplace, see page 28.

1

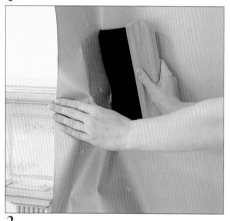

2

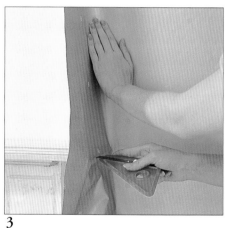

3

4

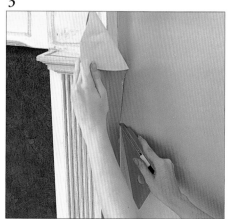

5

8

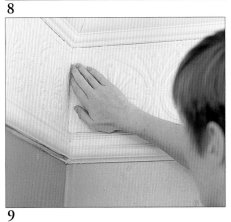

9

6

7

Day Two

Step 6

Begin by preparing the frieze, as shown on pages 36–7. Hang one length, and trim into the corners. Work from left to right, holding the frieze in concertina folds in your right hand as you unfold it. When hanging the second length, push one end of the frieze into the corner, allowing the end to overlap onto the return wall.

Step 7

Press a short straightedge into the corner to make an indent in the paper.

Step 8

Lift the paper away from the corner and cut along the indentation with the scissors.

Step 9

Push the paper firmly back into the corner. Continue hanging the frieze around the room in the same way.

Using wallpaper on a screen and the floor

Uncarpeted floors can be very appealing, but a wide expanse of empty floor can sometimes look too bland. Add an interesting feature to a vacant area by using strips of wallpaper to create a colourful rug effect.

Although wallpaper is not often seen on floors, in the right place it can create a stunning impression. If you would really like to have an ethnic rug, for example, but cannot afford it, or if you just want something unusual to brighten up a dull area, then once again wallpaper offers a range of attractive solutions.

How practical this is will of course depend on the type and condition of the floor, and the amount of wear and tear that the area in question is exposed to. It is pointless to use paper in a heavy-duty area, as no amount of protective varnish will keep the applied paper intact for long. In this case, or if the floor surface is too uneven for a large expanse of paper to look any good, try sticking a border around the edges of the room. This could either be a ready-made border or an improvised one.

For this project we chose to decorate a room in a Moroccan style. In addition to creating a 'rug', made out of strips cut from various wallpapers and borders, we also covered a plain wooden screen with wallpaper. Considerable care was needed to get the geometric design of the screen completely straight, but the results in both cases were very rewarding.

Planning your time

DAY ONE

AM: Prepare materials and wallpapers. Cut paper for screen

PM: Cover screen

DAY TWO

AM: Prepare materials. Measure floor area and cut paper to fit

PM: Cover floor with paper. Leave to dry then apply varnish

Tools and materials

Wallpaper

Wooden screen

Pasting table

Ruler

Pencil

Decorator's scissors

Wallpaper paste

Pasting brush

Bucket

Sponge

Wallpaper borders

Craft knife and blades

Tape measure

Paperhanger's brush

Yacht varnish

Varnish brush

1

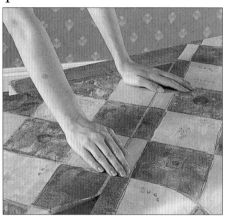

2

3

Day One

Step 1

Place the screen flat. Centre a piece of wall-paper on the screen. To use the paper diagonally, as pictured here, mark off the position of the diagonal lines in pencil on the screen. Paste and apply the paper to the screen, lining it up with the marked lines.

Step 2

Line up the next piece of paper with the diagonal line. Cut the paper to size, paste and attach to the screen.

Step 3

Finish covering the screen with a third piece. With all three pieces leave enough wallpaper to take around the edges of the screen.

Step 4

Measure, cut and paste the border. Mitre the corners, as shown on pages 38–9.

4

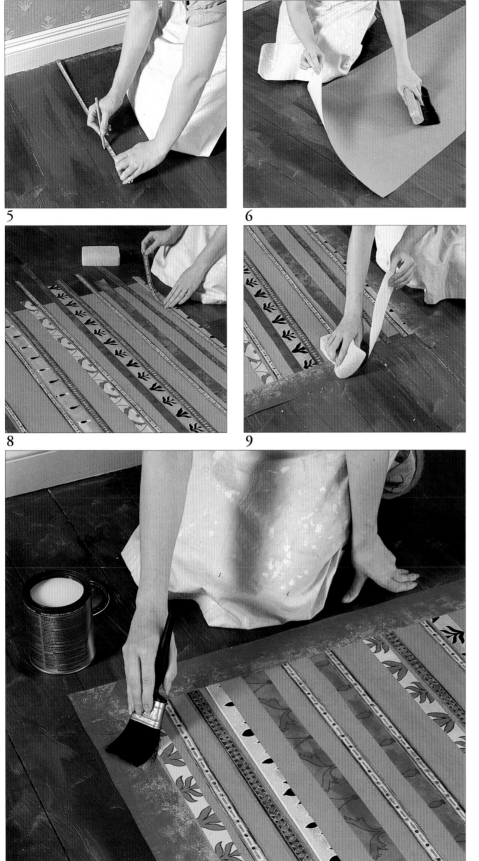

5

6

7

8

9

10

Day Two

Step 5

Choose a design and colours for the 'rug', then measure the area of the floor that you want to cover. Mark pencilled lines on the floor to act as guidelines.

Step 6

Make sure that the floor is clean before applying the paper. Cut the pieces of background wallpaper to fit, then paste and brush onto the floor.

Step 7

Lay various lengths of border loosely on top of the background paper in order to make a final decision on the pattern.

Step 8

Paste all the strips of border in their correct order, allowing a slight overlap at each end. Use a sponge to ensure a smooth finish.

Step 9

Apply a border round the four sides of the 'rug'. Here the border is the same as that used on the screen, to unify the overall look of the room.

Step 10

When dry, cover the wallpaper 'rug' with a hard-wearing yacht varnish. Follow the manufacturer's instructions, and allow the varnish to dry completely. Apply two or three further coats for added durability.

Wallpapering the ceiling and a door

If you want to create a room that is both casual and intimate, then take a tip from the French. The all-over look is not only charming but also good for disguising any unattractive features.

This look, in which walls, ceiling and door panels are all papered uniformly, has long been very popular in France, where it is often associated with 'toile de Jouey' designs. This literally means 'fabric from Jouey' – a town south of Paris that is famous for its textile designs, mostly rural in theme and of great charm. In addition to the wallpapers, matching and co-ordinating fabrics are also produced to extend the all-enveloping theme.

Most homes usually have at least one room which seems to defy improvement because it has, for example, a sloping ceiling or irregular or unbalanced corners and recesses. In such rooms the 'all over' look could well be the best solution, as its unifying effect will disguise a multitude of irregularities. In the same way, unattractive items such as mediocre cupboards and boxed-in pipes can be made much less obtrusive if they are covered over with wallpaper.

Above all, this approach also tends to produce a casual, informal style of room. It can be ideal, depending on the choice of wallpaper, for any space from a bathroom or a child's bedroom to a homely sitting-room.

This project will show you how to paper the ceiling, and offers advice on how to cut the paper neatly around a ceiling rose. If working on a ceiling, make sure that you have a stable platform from which to work. The best platform is created from trestles and planks, preferably long enough to allow you to walk the entire width of the ceiling while applying one length of paper.

Planning your time

DAY ONE

AM: Prepare materials. Measure and mark ceiling

PM: Hang the wallpaper on the ceiling up to the ceiling rose

DAY TWO

AM: Paper around the ceiling rose. Complete papering ceiling

PM: Paper door panels

Tools and materials

Trestles and planks

Wallpaper

Tape measure

Pencil

Straightedge

Wallpaper paste

Pasting table

Pasting brush

Bucket

Spare roll of wallpaper

Paperhanger's brush

Craft knife and blades

Day One

Step 1

Prepare and line the walls and ceiling. When wallpapering the ceiling, always paper across the longest dimension of the room. Begin by measuring away from the wall with a steel tape measure, marking off a distance of about 2.5cm (1in) less than the width of the wallpaper (see page 34) to allow for an overlap onto the wall. Make marks on the ceiling at this distance at various points, then join up the marks with a straightedge and pencil.

Step 2

Measure the length of the ceiling, and cut the paper, allowing a little extra at each end for trimming. Paste and soak the first length, then apply it to the ceiling, lining up the edge of the paper with the marked line. Hold the paper concertina style, as pictured, and offer up the pasted side to the ceiling. If you do not have anyone helping you, then use an extra roll of paper to support the concertina.

Step 3

Place the paper on the ceiling, lining up the edge with this line, and brush back with your left hand towards the cornice. Hold the remaining wallpaper, supported with a spare roll of paper, in your right hand.

Step 4

Continue hanging this length, working from left to right across the ceiling, unfolding the paper and brushing it into place. Use the brush to push the paper firmly into the cornice and corners.

Step 5

Return to the back wall, and trim away the overlap of paper, cutting into the angle between the cornice and the ceiling with a craft knife. Trim on the other two sides. Continue until you reach the ceiling rose (for further information on papering around ceiling fittings, see page 32).

1

3

2

4

5

6

7

8

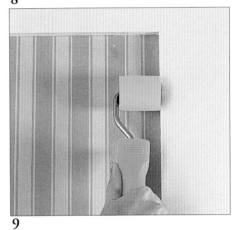

9

Day Two

Step 6

Apply a length of paper to the ceiling, allowing it to cover the ceiling rose. Push the paper into the edge of the rose, then use a craft knife to make several cuts in the paper to the edge of the ceiling rose.

Step 7

Trim off the resulting rectangular overlaps of paper with the knife, then smooth the paper firmly onto the ceiling around the rose.

Step 8

To paper the door panel, place the paper over the panel and using a pencil, mark out the area on the paper. Allow a small overlap to work into the edges of the panel.

Step 9

Cut and paste the paper and hang in the panel, then roll it into place and trim.

Finishing decorative items with wallpaper

It is not only flat surfaces that can be transformed with wallpaper. Use scraps of wallpaper to breathe new life into all kinds of household objects and to create numerous decorative gifts for family and friends.

W e all have items in our homes which are bland or boring, or which have seen better days. If you do not wish to replace them – perhaps they are old friends – then why not freshen them up or add more interest to them by partly or wholly covering them in wallpaper?

Lampshades, table mats, waste paper baskets, trays and tables are just a few of the objects which can be made over in this way. In fact almost any item can be covered with wallpaper as long as the surface is well prepared and, where necessary, the paper is heavily protected with lacquer or varnish.

Striking effects can also be obtained by cutting out images from wallpapers and pasting them either straight on to items or on to surfaces that have first been covered with another paper or even painted.

For our project we chose a children's toy box and a lampshade. Covering a round object such as a lampshade is one of the trickier papering jobs, but matching or co-ordinating lampshades within an overall decorative scheme can be an extremely effective feature. The illustration opposite also shows some attractively papered hat boxes and an umbrella stand.

Planning your time

DAY ONE

AM: Prepare materials. Measure lampshade and cut paper to fit

PM: Cover lampshade

DAY TWO

AM: Prepare materials. Measure toy box and cut paper to fit

PM: Cover toy box

Tools and materials

Wallpaper

Lampshade

Toy box

Tape measure

Pasting table

Craft knife and blades

Straightedge

Wallpaper paste

Pasting brush

Bucket

Sponge

Spirit level

Small offcut of wood

Day One: lampshade

Step 1

Choose some wallpaper to decorate a lampshade, perhaps to match or co-ordinate with the paper or fabric used in a particular room. Measure the diameter and height of the lampshade. Unroll the paper on the pasting table, then use a craft knife and straightedge to cut a piece of paper to fit around the lampshade. Make sure that the design on the wallpaper is applied the right way up. The paper used here had a vertical design, so two pieces of paper were needed to wrap round the diameter of the shade.

Step 2

Take a second piece of the same paper and line it up next to the first piece, matching the design exactly. Cut the paper to fit the other side of the shade.

Step 3

Paste and soak the paper, then place the first piece around half the lampshade, and sponge it in position.

Step 4

Add the second bit of wallpaper to the other side of the lampshade, placing it carefully to match the design on the first piece. Sponge in place, then trim the paper around the top and bottom of the lampshade with a craft knife.

1

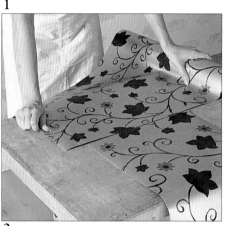

2

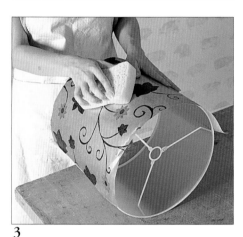

3

4

The finishing touch

Wallpaper can be used to line drawers, cupboards and boxes, and even for découpage projects. This is a Victorian technique, involving decorating a surface with cut-out paper images. The finished surface is then built up with several coats of varnish to create a hand-painted look.

1

3

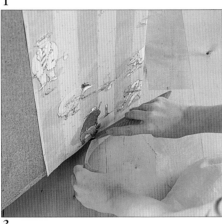

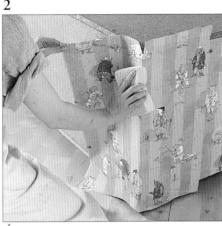

4

5

Day Two: toy box

Step 1

Choose a brightly coloured paper to cover a child's toy box. Mark a vertical line in pencil down one side of the box with a spirit level and then a straightedge. Measure the box and cut enough paper to cover the box, making sure to allow extra paper for trimming.

Step 2

Paste and soak the first piece of paper. Line one side up with the marked line on the box, and apply it to the box, smoothing it in place with a sponge.

Step 3

Use a craft knife to trim the paper to the edges of the box at the top and bottom.

Step 4

Line up the next piece of paper with the first piece and apply it to the box, wrapping it round the corner.

Step 5

Cover the top or lid of the box with paper. Line up the paper so that it is straight. Cut to size, allowing enough to wrap over the edge and under the lid. Trim the paper to fit at the corners. Use an offcut of wood to hold the lid open while working on it.

Glossary

Craft knife

Paperhanger's brush

Pasting brush

Adhesive

Adhesive is the overall term for the paste which is used to stick the numerous varieties of wallpaper and wallcoverings to walls and ceilings. Always use the type of adhesive recommended by the manufacturer of the wallpaper that you are using.

Artist's brushes

Available in different sizes, a small artist's brush is ideal for applying extra paste to overlapping or lifting seams.

Butt or butt joint

When two pieces of wallpaper are hung on the wall and the edges are gently pushed together, this is known as a butt joint. It is most important that the edges touch, without leaving a gap or creating an overlap.

Concertina

For ease of handling, long lengths of pasted wallpaper should be folded concertina style in order to be put up on ceilings or hung horizontally around a room. Occasionally very long, vertical drops of paper are folded in this way as well, for example when papering on a staircase.

Cornice

The cornice is the continuous, horizontal moulding which runs around a room, just below the ceiling. Cornices are available in a variety of depths and types of moulding. Care should be taken when choosing a new cornice to ensure that it is the correct depth for the room.

Craft or trimming knife

Craft knives are excellent for trimming and cutting paper around wall fittings and at difficult angles, for example when mitring a corner. A craft knife should have retractable and replaceable blades. Care should be taken as the blades are extremely sharp. Craft knives are sometimes combined with a short straightedge.

Dado or dado rail

The dado is the lower part of a wall, separated from the top part by a wooden rail known as a dado rail.

Decorator's scissors

The blades of decorator's scissors are much longer than standard scissors. The ends of the blades are also specially shaped, allowing the scissors to make creases in the paper without actually tearing the paper.

Filler and filling knife

Used when preparing walls for papering. Fillers are thick pastes that can be smoothed into cracks or holes in a wall using a strong, flat knife. The filler hardens as it dries and can be sanded smooth.

Paperhanger's brush

Wide brushes with a wooden handle, available in various sizes. The bristles are soft and thick. Paperhanger's brushes are used for smoothing down the wallpaper, and brushing out any bubbles, when it is hung on the wall and ceiling.

Pasting brush

It is possible to use a standard paint brush to apply paste to wallpaper, but in order to get a much better and more even spread of paste, it is preferable to use a proprietary pasting brush. The bristles are sturdier and more flexible than standard paint brushes.

Pasting table

Collapsible wooden tables that are easy to carry about. Pasting tables are not expensive, and because the tables are only slightly wider than an average roll of wallpaper, they make the task of pasting the wallpaper much easier.

Plumb line

A small weight attatched to a length of string. A plumb line is used to make a an accurate vertical line on a wall, ensuring that the first length of wallpaper will be hung perfectly straight.

Seam roller

A rolling tool with a 3cm (1¼in) wide head. When using wallpaper or embossed papers, use a roller with a rubber or felt head, so it will not flatten the edges of the paper or the design. When hanging vinyls and borders, it is possible to use a seam roller with a head made of plastic or wood.

Size

Usually a diluted wallpaper paste, size should be applied to the walls after they have been cleaned and lined. It aids the adhesion of the wallpaper and gives better 'slip', allowing greater flexibility when positioning the paper on the wall.

Spirit level

Made from wood or metal, spirit levels contain a small glass tube in which there is an air bubble. If the bubble appears in the centre of the tube, then the spirit level is straight. They are used to make sure that, when hanging horizontal paper or borders, the paper is absolutely straight. They can also be used vertically.

Steam stripper

A machine used to ease the process of stripping wallpaper from walls. Available to buy or hire, there are several models available. Always follow the manufacturer's instructions for use.

Stepladder

It is necessary to have a good stepladder when hanging wallpaper, so you can reach the ceiling or cornice with ease. If working on a staircase ensure that the stepladder has rubber pads on its feet so that it will not slip.

Straightedge

This is a length of metal, available in various widths and lengths. A straightedge usually has measurements marked on it. They are especially useful when cutting through an overlap or two pieces of wallpaper. They also help when drawing horizontal lines around a room.

Tape measure

Steel tape measures are used for measuring heights and distances around rooms, as well as for making smaller measurements while decorating. They are available in various lengths and have the advantage that they are very flexible, especially round corners.

Trestle platform

When papering a ceiling you will need to construct a platform, either with two stepladders or two trestles and some planks.

Wire brush

A brush with stiff, wire bristles, that is used to rough up wallpaper on a wall before soaking the paper with water in order to strip it from the wall.

Plumb line

Seam roller

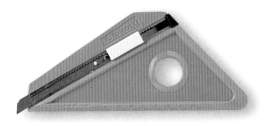

Short straightedge and knife

Suppliers

The author and publishers would like to thank the following suppliers:

WALLPAPERS, BORDERS AND FABRICS

Akzo Nobel Decorative Coatings Ltd
P.O. Box 37
Crown House
Hollins Road
Darwen
Lancashire
BB3 0BG
Tel. 01254 704951
(*Anaglypta border in the Papering a fireplace and hanging a frieze project, pages 60–63*)

Cole & Son (Wallpaper) Ltd
Talbot House
17 Church Street
Rickmansworth
Hertfordshire
WD3 1DE
Tel. 01923 710041
(*Wallpaper in the Papering a staircase with sloping walls project, pages 48–51*)

Crowson Fabrics Ltd
Crowson House
Bellbrook Park
Uckfield
East Sussex
TN22 1OZ
Tel. 01825 761044
(*Yellow background wallpaper in the Creating a set on design in a hallway project, pages 56–9*)

S.J. Dixon & Son Ltd
Dixon House
Cleveland Road
Wolverhampton
WV2 1BX
Tel. 01902 452491
(*Black and grey wallpaper in the Creating a set on design in a hallway project, pages 56–9*)

Dixon Turner Wallcoverings Ltd
Madoc Works
Henfaes Lane
Welshpool
Montgomeryshire
SY21 7BE
Tel. 01938 552671
(*Wallpaper on lampshade in the Finishing decorative items with wallpaper project, pages 72–5*)

Harlequin Fabrics and Wallpapers Ltd
Cossington Road
Sileby
Loughborough
Leicestershire
LE12 7RU
Tel. 01509 816575
(*Wallpaper in the Using two papers and hanging into a corner project, pages 44–7*)

Hill & Knowles
Kew Limited Palace of Industry
Olympic Way,
Wembley
Middlesex
HA9 0DB
Tel. 0208 900 1333
(*Wallpapers and fabrics used in the Using wallpaper on a screen and the floor project, pages 64–7*)

Jab Anstoetz
1/15–16 1st Floor Centre Dome
Chelsea Harbour Design Centre
Chelsea Harbour
London
SW10 0XE
Tel. 0207 349 9323
(Green and silver fabrics in the Hanging
wallpaper horizontally project, pages 52–5)

Nouveau Fabrics Ltd
Queen's Road
Doncaster
South Yorkshire
DN1 2NH
Tel. 01302 329601
(Wallpaper in the Wallpapering the ceiling
and a door project, pages 68–71)

Osborne & Little plc
49 Temperley Road
London
SW12 8QE
Tel. 0208 675 2255
(Wallpaper on all items except the
lampshade in the Finishing decorative items
with wallpaper project, pages 72–5)

Arthur Sanderson & Sons Ltd
100 Acres
Sanderson Road
Uxbridge
Middlesex
UB8 1DH
Tel. 01895 238244
(Silver paper in the Hanging wallpaper
horizontally project and the gold paper in
the Papering a fireplace and hanging a frieze
project, pages 60–3)

Sixten & Cassey Ltd
Crookley Park
Blendworth
Waterlooville
Hampshire
PO8 0AD
Tel. 01705 592000
(Green wallpaper in the Hanging
wallpaper horizontally project, pages 52–5)

PAINTS

Ottilie Stevenson Ltd
4 Charlotte Road
London
EC2A 3DH
Tel. 0207 739 7321

ADHESIVES

C.Brewer & Sons Ltd
327 Putney Bridge Road
Putney
London
SW15 2PG
Tel. 0208 788 9335

Lines of Pinner
26 High Street.
Pinner
Middlesex
HA5 5PW
Tel. 0208 429 0939

Ray Munn Ltd
861–863 Fulham Road
London
SW6 5HP
Tel. 0207 384 3723

Ward Bekker Sales Ltd
Northgate
White Lund Estate
Morecambe
Lancashire
LA3 3PA
Tel. 01524 63233/33466

GENERAL ACKNOWLEDGEMENTS

Designers Selection Ltd
P.O. Box 81
Grantham
Lincolnshire
NG31 8FN
Tel. 01476 579555

Monkwell Ltd
10–12 Wharfdale Road
Bournemouth
Dorset
BH4 9BT
Tel. 01202 752944

Peter Topp Interiors
343 Fulham Palace Road
London
SW6 6TD
Tel. 0207 736 4821

The Wallfashion Bureau
High Corn Mill
Chapel Hill
Skipton
North Yorkshire
BD23 1NL
Tel. 01756 790 730

Index